MARTIN
LUTHER
KING, JR.

MARTIN LUTHER KING, JR.

Jean Darby

Lerner Publications Company • Minneapolis

Front and back cover photographs are by Flip Schulke.

This book is available in two editions:
Library binding by Lerner Publications Company,
    a division of Lerner Publishing Group
Soft cover by First Avenue Editions,
    an imprint of Lerner Publishing Group
241 First Avenue North
Minneapolis, MN 55401 U.S.A.

Website address: www.lernerbooks.com

Library of Congress Cataloging-in-Publication Data

Darby, Jean.
    Martin Luther King / by Jean Darby.
        p.   cm.
    Includes bibliographical references.
    Summary: A biography of the civil rights leader whose philosophy and practice of nonviolent civil disobedience helped American blacks win many battles for equal rights.
    ISBN 0-8225-4902-6 (lib. bdg. : alk. paper)
    ISBN 0-8225-9611-3 (pbk. : alk. paper)
    1. King, Martin Luther, Jr., 1929–1968 —Juvenile literature. 2. Afro-Americans—Biography—Juvenile literature. 3. Baptist—United States—Clergy—Biography—Juvenile literature. 4. Civil rights workers—United States—Biography—Juvenile literature. 5. Afro-Americans—Civil rights—Juvenile literature. 6. Nonviolence—Religious aspect—Baptist—Juvenile literature. [1. Martin Luther King, Jr., 1929–1968 2. Clergy. 3. Afro-Americans—Biography 4. Afro-Americans—Civil rights.] I. Title.
E185.97.K5D29   1989   1990
323.92—dc20   89–36797

Manufactured in the United States of America
5 6 7 8 9 10 – JR – 06 05 04 03 02 01

Contents

∽ ONE ∽

Growing Up Black
1929-1944

*"Don't let this thing make you feel you're not as good
as white people. You're as good as anyone else,
and don't you forget it."*
—Alberta King

Martin Luther King, Jr., came quietly into the
world on a cold, cloudy Saturday morning, January 15, 1929.
When the second child of Alberta and Martin Luther King,
Sr., was born, he lay so still that the doctor thought he would
not live. But after several vigorous slaps on his bottom, the
baby cried. No one knew it then, but this newborn child
would one day lead the way from unjust treatment that was
a kind of slavery to a way of life that offered freedom,
justice, and dignity for all people.

The King family lived in a gray and white frame house
at 501 Auburn Avenue. From Peachtree Street, then a street
for white people, Auburn sloped down in one direction toward
the bustling black business district in downtown Atlanta,
Georgia. In the opposite direction, it rose on a hill to a
community of houses and fine churches. Martin's family was

From the pulpit in Ebenezer Baptist Church, Martin Luther King, Sr., preached the worth of black people.

respected in the black community. His father was a minister, and from the pulpit he preached about the worth of black people, telling them to be strong and brave. He tried to protect his daughter and two sons from the insults and abuses of the white population, but it was not always possible. When Martin Luther King was growing up, many things happened to black people in the South that were not only unjust, but also confusing and frightening.

On one bright, sunny day, Martin skipped across the street to play with his friends, sons of the neighborhood grocer. After he knocked, it seemed to take longer than usual for anyone to open the door. When it was opened finally, his friend's mother seemed to be looking at him in a strange way, and her voice had a slightly different tone. "You boys are old enough for school now," she said. "You can't play here anymore."

Ebenezer Baptist Church in Atlanta, Georgia

Bewildered by the sudden change in the way his friend's mother treated him, Martin hurried home to his own mother. "Why can't I play over there anymore?" he asked.

His mother knelt down and held him close. She knew that what she had to say would hurt her son, and it hurt her to have to tell him. She pressed her cheek against his and tried to explain. "You are black. Your friend is white." Then, holding him even tighter, she said, "Don't let this thing impress you. Don't let it make you feel you're not as good as white people. You're as good as anyone else, and don't you forget it."

Martin was too young to understand completely the meaning of her words, but the message they gave him was clear: Blacks were different from whites, and he was black.

Martin Luther King, Jr., fourth from right, *at a birthday party*

Martin soon learned to read signs that said NO COLORED ALLOWED. WHITES ONLY. Sometimes he looked down at his hands and examined them. He wondered what was wrong with being black.

Black people could not eat where white people ate or attend the same movie theaters. They had to eat at "colored" restaurants, and they had to go to the shabby "colored" theaters, where faded films fluttered on the screen. Black children had to attend schools that were run-down and poorly equipped. They could not drink from the same water fountains as whites or buy Cokes where white children bought theirs. And black people had to ride in the back of the bus. Sometimes they could not ride on a bus at all. Martin had heard about one frightening bus incident.

When a small black child tried to get on a bus, the driver told him to drop his money in the box. The child did as he was told. Then he was ordered to go to the back of the bus.

The small boy jumped down from the bus to go around to the back door. He ran as fast as he could, but before he could reach the door, the wheels of the bus spun in the gravel, and it took off without him. The small, would-be passenger had lost both his pennies and his ride.

The bus system brought unhappiness to black people, and shopping was no better. One day when Martin and his mother were in a department store, he looked across the room and saw an elevator with fancy trim and shiny buttons to push. "Why don't we ride over there?" he asked. "Shush!" his mother said as she took his arm. "Those elevators are for white people. We must ride here." Martin's eyes filled with tears. The freight elevator that they had to ride was not nearly as exciting as those across the room. Another time, a white woman screamed, "That little nigger stepped on my toe!" and she slapped Martin across the face. More and more, the safe, orderly life Martin had known as a very small child began to crumble, and it no longer seemed so secure.

Although anger began to build up inside Martin, his father worked diligently to set a positive example of self-esteem. On one occasion when Martin was riding in the car with his father, a policeman signaled them to pull over. "All right, boy," the officer said in a menacing tone. Without flinching, the pastor said, "I'm no boy." Pointing to Martin, he said, "This is a boy. I am a man."

Not long afterward, Martin and his father went into a shoe store and sat in chairs near the door. "What do you think you're doing?" the angry clerk asked. "You know you can't sit there."

Martin felt uncomfortable. He lowered his eyes and fiddled with his fingers.

*Martin's parents,
Alberta Williams
King and Martin
Luther King, Sr.*

"I see nothing wrong with these seats," Martin's father answered.

The clerk's lips began to quiver. "It's a rule! The colored sit at the back!"

"We'll buy shoes sitting here," Rev. King said, "or we won't buy shoes at all." He took Martin by the hand, and they left.

Even though Martin was learning his "place" as a black child in Atlanta, Georgia, there was also a good side to his life. He lived in a middle-class family. He never suffered from hunger or cold. He had plenty of warm clothes and nourishing food. He lived in a nice house. And, best of all, the grandmother he loved so much lived with them.

Martin also loved Ebenezer Baptist Church, where his father preached and where Martin learned the Scriptures.

During church services, he sat in the family pew with his grandmother, his older sister, Christine, and his brother, Alfred Daniel (called A.D.). From there, Martin looked up at his father, who occupied a tall wooden chair in front of a gold cross. Just over to the side, his mother sat at the organ and played music for the service. The worship service was loud and lively, with people singing, clapping hands, and dancing in the aisles. When his father spoke, it was with a passion that caused tears to flow from the eyes of parishioners. Their excited voices chanted, "Amen! Yes! That's right, brother!"

After the worship service, Sunday dinner was held at the church. Tables were filled with fried chicken, ham, black-eyed peas, and watermelon. When Martin was only six, he sang hymns at these gatherings. He stood on a table and bellowed, "I want to be more like Jesus."

People who knew Martin came to realize that he was not an ordinary child. "He's brilliant," church members would whisper to one another. "Have you noticed how he talks? Such big words!" And Martin did not disappoint his admirers.

He began reading at an early age. His favorite books were about black history and the people who made it. He read about Frederick Douglass and Harriet Tubman, slaves who escaped to freedom. He read about Booker T. Washington, who founded the first college for blacks. And he learned how George Washington Carver, through his research, developed many products from peanuts. Stretched out on his bed, Martin read stories of Paul Robeson, the singer, Joe Louis, the boxer, and Jesse Owens, the Olympic gold-medal winner. Martin was such a good student that he skipped ninth grade and caught up with his sister, Christine, who was a year older.

When World War II started, so many young men went into the army and navy that colleges didn't have enough

Martin Luther King in front of his boyhood home on Auburn Avenue in Atlanta, Georgia

students to fill the classrooms. They needed to build their enrollment. Some schools decided to solve the problem by admitting exceptional high school students. When Martin was only 15, he passed a college entrance exam, and, in September 1944, he followed a family tradition by entering Morehouse College in Atlanta.

In many ways he was a typical teenager. He was so fond of clothes that his friends nicknamed him "Tweed."

"How do I look?" he asked his friends, as he strutted in front of them.

They laughed and told him, "You're okay, Tweed."

He liked girls and loved loud music. He also liked to dance, and this ultimately brought him trouble. When his father, who didn't approve of dancing, learned that his son had been attending dances, he made Martin apologize in front of the entire church congregation.

What Martin loved even more than dancing was the sense of freedom on the Morehouse campus. College provided him with the opportunity to talk freely about the evils of racial segregation, the practice of separating people according to the color of their skin. He said, "The professors... encouraged us... and for the first time in my life, I realized that nobody there was afraid." A friend of Martin's recalled, "We used to sit up way into the morning discussing the social issues of the day." These occasions eventually led Martin to waver in his plan for the future.

✑ TWO ✑

Beyond Jim Crow
1944-1955

"Injustice anywhere is a threat to justice everywhere."
—Martin Luther King, Jr.

During the summer before Martin entered Morehouse, he and his brother worked in Connecticut as tobacco pickers. Several high-school and college students were in the group. Most of the students worked there out of a sense of adventure more than need. They wanted to see what life was like in a different part of the country. It was a happy experience for Martin, because in the North there were no Jim Crow laws separating the races. (Jim Crow laws were practices that limited the rights of black people. The term came into use in the 1880s and originally referred to a black character in an old song.)

In Connecticut, Martin could buy Cokes where his white friends bought theirs, and he could ride in the front of the bus. He could sit at any lunch counter he chose. Restrooms were not segregated. There were no WHITES ONLY signs.

It was the first time since he started school that he was allowed to have white friends. Through talking with them, Martin came to believe that the white race was not the problem in the South. The problem was racial segregation. Martin Luther King was still quite young when he decided that all people were equal, and people of all races should be able to live in the same neighborhoods, work together on the same jobs, and use the same drinking fountains, hotels, and restaurants.

Martin lived at home while he went to college. His freshman adviser remembered him as "quiet, introspective, and very much introverted...." During his freshman year, Martin had told his father that he wanted to be a lawyer or a doctor. But, while studying at Morehouse, he changed his mind. Martin listened to many new ideas—ideas that were to have a lasting impact on his life. The professors there taught a "social gospel" that was different from the theatrical church services that he had known as a child.

As time went on, he found his ideal in two Morehouse ministers, Dr. George D. Kelsey, director of the religion department, and Dr. Benjamin E. Mays, the college president. In his junior year, influenced by these two outstanding men, Martin decided to become a minister. His love for the church took precedence over all other choices.

"Dad," he said, "I have come to see that God has placed a responsibility on my shoulders. I'm going to be a preacher."

In 1948, when Martin was 19, he graduated with a bachelor of arts degree from Morehouse College and enrolled as a divinity student in Crozer Theological Seminary in Chester, Pennsylvania. It was his first opportunity to live alone and away from the powerful influence of his father. In his new, racially integrated school, Martin tried to overcome

King, right, *attended Crozer Theological Seminary,* above.

Mohandas Gandhi had a strong influence on King's belief in nonviolent resistance.

what he believed to be the white people's stereotype of blacks —always late, loud, laughing, and messy. As a result, Martin was overly serious, overdressed, and spotlessly neat about his clothes and room. If he was even a minute late for class, he thought everyone noticed it. Martin took his studying seriously, attending class during the day and studying far into the night.

"Hey, Tweed," his friends would call. "Turn off your light."

Martin would shake his head and tell them, "You go to sleep. I'm on the track of something important."

In his book *Stride Toward Freedom,* Martin Luther King wrote, "Not until I entered Crozer Theological Seminary... did I begin a serious intellectual quest for a method to eliminate social evil." Even as a young man, he wanted to make the world a better place for all people. As a divinity student, Martin studied the beliefs of many philosophers, including

Hegel, Walter Rauschenbusch, Reinhold Niebuhr, Paul Tillich, and Mohandas Gandhi.

In 1950, Martin went to hear a lecture by Dr. Mordecai Johnson, president of Howard University. Dr. Johnson had just returned from India. He talked about his travels and about Gandhi's spiritual leadership. Mohandas Gandhi believed in nonviolent resistance. Martin was somewhat familiar with Gandhi's successful attempt to free India from British rule, an effort that had begun long before Martin was born and had lasted for 30 years. Instead of fighting against the British with guns, Gandhi had used techniques such as fasts, boycotts, general strikes, large marches, and civil disobedience. He preached the idea of returning good for evil, of openly disobeying certain laws, and willingly paying the penalty for doing so. "I want to teach your hearts," Gandhi said to his enemies. "Only then will you change." Martin Luther King was impressed with what he heard, but he was not at all sure that such techniques would work in the United States.

In 1951, King graduated from Crozer with the highest grade point average in his class. He won the Plafker Award for most outstanding student and received the J. Lewis Crozer fellowship to study at a university of his choice. His parents gave him a hug and a brand-new Chevrolet car.

The following September, Martin enrolled as a graduate student in philosophy at Boston University. He continued to study the works of the philosophers and theologians with whom he had become familiar at Crozer.

With every page he read, his curiosity grew. His constant search for answers fed his imagination. He was alert and eager. He was strong and restless. Someday all these qualities would work together for him. In the meantime, he studied at

Coretta Scott King planned to be a famous singer when she finished school.

Boston University during the day and then drove across the Charles River to attend additional philosophy and theology classes at Harvard University.

Martin was bright and good-looking. He hoped to meet a wife with four qualities: a strong character, intelligence, a good personality, and beauty. A friend had told him to call Coretta Scott. Coretta fit the description, but she had no intention of marrying a Baptist minister. A graduate of Antioch College, Coretta was studying voice at the New England Conservatory of Music. She pictured herself traveling across the country on concert tours, performing before audiences, and taking curtain calls. Friends advised her not to sacrifice her art for a glamourless life with a preacher, but one date led to another, and eventually she fell in love with Martin. They were married on June 18, 1953, in Marion, Alabama, Coretta's home. After the honeymoon, the couple moved into an apartment near the conservatory.

When Martin finished the classes he needed for his degree, he began to look for a job. After considering several possibilities, he accepted the position of minister at Dexter Avenue Baptist Church in Montgomery, Alabama. Martin traveled to Montgomery on weekends and then returned to Boston, where Coretta was completing her studies. After experiencing life in the North, the Kings did not want to return to the South where blacks were discriminated against, but Martin felt that it was his duty to return. He was needed there. "We will only stay a short time," he told Coretta.

In the spring of 1955, Martin finished writing his thesis (a required essay), and on June 5, he was awarded a doctorate degree (Ph.D.) in theology and became Dr. Martin Luther King.

Martin graduated with a Ph.D. in theology from Boston University.

It was an exciting day for the King family. Martin had reached a goal that few black people had reached before him. He felt satisfied. He knew he was moving forward. He was gaining knowledge and respect. And although he wasn't aware of it then, he was on his way to something great.

On May 31 of that same year, the Supreme Court ruled that schools were to be desegregated "with all deliberate speed." White southerners were shocked. "Blacks go to school with whites?" They vented their anger in newspapers, on radio and television, and to their local government leaders. "We will not have our children in schools with niggers!" They were not only worried about what would happen to the scholastic standings of their schools, they were also worried that people of different races would become friends. They might even marry! White Citizens Councils, similar to the Ku Klux Klan, sprang up in the South. The atmosphere turned explosive. Because of the way white people felt and acted, the Court's decision had little effect in Montgomery. Black and white children continued to go to separate schools, but pressure continued to grow. Black people were tired of suffering indignities. They were tired of riding in the back of the bus. They were tired of white drivers yelling, "Hey, nigger." They were tired of the other cruel and unfair treatment they received.

Then, on August 28, an act of violence occurred that shocked the black community. Emmet Till, a 14-year-old Chicago boy who was visiting relatives near Money, Mississippi, was kidnapped and lynched (hanged). Black people were outraged, but they had little power to do anything. Their anger had no outlet, but it continued to grow over the next few months.

Dexter Avenue Baptist Church in Montgomery, Alabama

Thursday, December 1, was an unusually warm day in Montgomery, Alabama. Rosa Parks climbed on a bus to go to her job as a seamstress at a department store. Rosa was a quiet, dignified woman who worked hard and did well at her job. After work, the streets were crowded with Christmas shoppers and workers on their way home. Rosa, like the other passengers, was tired from her day's work. She boarded the bus to go home and found a seat just behind the white section. Rosa leaned back in the seat as the bus bumped along.

When the bus pulled up to the Empire Theater stop, six white people got on. The bus driver, J. F. Blake, got up to ask the black riders just behind the white section to give up their seats for the white passengers. The practice was common

In the South, black passengers sat behind white people and had to give up their seats if white people were standing.

and happened every day, often with threats or blows from the driver. Three black passengers stood up immediately, but Rosa didn't move. Unlike many drivers, Blake did not use violence or crude language, especially in the presence of white female passengers. He again asked Rosa to give up her seat, and again she refused. She sat motionless. She had made up her mind. She was going to stay seated.

The driver then called the police. Two patrolmen took Rosa to the police station, where she was booked for violating the city bus ordinance. Her quiet dignity during the arrest and arraignment helped focus public attention on the single charge of refusing to give up a seat to a white person on a public bus. There had been no disorderly conduct, no drunkenness—none of the charges police and bus drivers frequently made up as the cause for arrest. Rosa's case was clear. It was what black leaders had been waiting for. Now they could go to court to test the law. Her quiet defiance happened at just the right moment in history.

At the police station, she wasn't allowed a drink of water, as the fountain was for whites only, but she was allowed to make a telephone call. She phoned E. D. Nixon, who was a fearless and influential leader in the black community. Mr. Nixon was away when the call came, but his wife took the message. As soon as he returned and got Rosa's message, he went to the police station and arranged for her release.

Rosa Parks, above, *refused to give up her seat on the bus. The Montgomery bus boycott developed from her brave act.*

↭ THREE ↭

Chosen to Lead

1955

"We can no longer lend our cooperation to an evil system."
—Martin Luther King, Jr.

News of Rosa Parks's arrest spread from house to house and from office to office. Throughout the black community, telephones buzzed with her story. People felt that this time something should be done.

Mr. Nixon talked with several ministers and civic leaders, and they agreed that the time had come to insist on change. But how? How could black people obtain equal rights on buses? What nonviolent action could they take?

Finally the group decided to organize a boycott. If the black people of Montgomery refused to ride the buses, the bus company would lose about 75 percent of its business. Maybe if the company began to fail, it would listen to the black people.

About 45 ministers and civic leaders called a meeting on Friday, December 2, to talk about this exciting plan. They

---

had to decide how to organize the boycott so that it would work. To make the boycott successful, the leaders would have to make sure that all the black people in Montgomery knew about it and were willing to work together. They felt this action would bring power to black people, but they also realized it would bring hardship, since many people who had to get to work did not own cars. The boycott was a peaceful but powerful way of sending a message to the bus company. When the meeting ended, King leaned back in his chair and looked toward the ceiling. "The clock on the wall says almost midnight," he said, "but the clock in our souls reveals that it is daybreak."

By late Friday afternoon, leaflets had been quickly printed and distributed. They read:

> Don't ride the bus to work, to town, to school, or any place Monday, December 5.

> Another Negro woman has been arrested and put in jail because she refused to give up her bus seat.

> Don't ride the buses to work, to town, to school, or anywhere on Monday. If you work, take a cab, or share a ride, or walk.

> Come to a mass meeting Monday at 7:00 P.M., at the Holt Street Baptist Church for further instructions.

When Martin first heard about the boycott, he wasn't sure it was a good idea. The bus line would lose money. Families of bus workers depended on money from the bus line for their food and clothing. He turned to his books, searched his heart, and prayed to God for answers to these problems. After wrestling with his thoughts, Martin came to the conclusion that his "brothers" were not trying to hurt anyone. Instead, they were refusing to cooperate with an unfair system. He could go along with that idea.

Black people in Montgomery welcomed the news of the boycott, but would they would really support it? On Monday morning the weather might be cold or rainy. How many people would walk to work, carpool, or stay home from places where they really wanted to go? Men talked about it in barber shops, bars, and pool halls. The ladies of the Women's Political Council got on the telephone to spread the word. People encouraged each other, but they could not hide their fear. On Sunday, the boycott got front-page coverage in the citywide Montgomery *Advertiser*. Black ministers preached about it from their pulpits and emphasized the need for loyalty and self-sacrifice. After church, leaders continued to organize the community. They could not—must not—fail!

Coretta and Martin awoke earlier than usual on Monday morning. At 5:30 A.M. they were dressed and waiting to see the first bus pass their window at 6:00 A.M. Martin went into the kitchen to make a cup of coffee. In the living room, Coretta held back the lace curtain and anxiously waited for the bus to come rumbling down the hill. Would it be full? How many people would be riding? Was the boycott going to be a success? Finally, the bus appeared.

"Martin! Martin! Come quick."

Martin put down his coffee and ran to the living room.

They leaned forward, peering through the pane.

"Do you see what I see, Martin?"

He paused. "Wait just one minute. Yes . . . . I think I do."

"The bus is empty, Martin. The bus is empty!"

Martin jumped into his car and cruised down every major street to examine each passing bus. Throughout the city, he saw only eight passengers. Some people rode mules. Others drove horse-drawn buggies. People with cars shared them.

Hundreds of people walked to show their commitment. A man in a car pulled up to an elderly woman.

"Jump in Grandmother," the driver invited. "You don't need to walk."

"I'm not walking for myself," the old woman said. "I'm walking for my children and grandchildren."

White citizens found it hard to believe the determination of the black community. "The niggers have goon squads," they cried. "They're forcing people away from the buses." Nothing could have been further from the truth. The black people were united. The boycott was on.

At 9:00 A.M., Dr. Martin Luther King and his friend Reverend Ralph Abernathy, pastor of the First Baptist Church, drove to city hall to attend Rosa Parks's trial. An angry crowd had gathered, filling the streets and sidewalks. Police stood guard with sawed-off shotguns, and a chill ran down Martin's spine. "They'd better not lose control of this one," he whispered to Reverend Abernathy.

Each person waited anxiously for the verdict. When the judge's gavel banged, the word *guilty* rang through the crowd. Most people were angry, but Martin Luther King was thinking ahead. "This decision may not be constitutional," he told Ralph Abernathy. "Now we can test it in a federal court."

Rosa Parks was fined $10 plus court costs. Her attorney, Fred Gray, immediately filed an appeal. Was segregation legal? The law would be tested.

Why did Rosa Parks remain seated on that particular day? Physically she was no more tired than usual at the end of a workday. However, she was tired of unfair treatment. Although Rosa did not think of herself as a courageous person, her brave act triggered the Montgomery boycott and inaugurated the civil rights era. Martin Luther King later said that Rosa had been "tracked down by the *zeitgeist* [pronounced ZITE-guyste], the spirit of the times." At last segregation was out in the open and under attack.

Late on Monday afternoon, the ministers from the black community met at one of the churches. The one-day boycott had been a success. Now they had to decide whether it should be continued. Summer days would be hot, and winter days got cold and windy. Sometimes it would rain. They wondered if people would get tired of the inconvenience and start riding the buses again because it was so much easier.

It didn't take long for them to decide. "The boycott must continue," Ralph Abernathy said.

"Yes, brother, you're right."

"We're making headway now. We mustn't stop."

They decided to carry on with the boycott. To organize the extended protest, they formed an organization called the Montgomery Improvement Association (MIA). Martin Luther King was elected president. The group wanted to continue the boycott until a few basic demands were met. These included:

1. Courteous treatment by bus drivers
2. A first-come, first-served seating arrangement, with blacks filling the bus from the back to the front and whites from the front to the back
3. Employment of black drivers on predominantly black routes

Before they adjourned, the members of the new association decided that Martin should give a speech at the mass meeting that was going to be held at the Holt Street Baptist Church that evening. Rosa Parks would also speak.

On the way home, Martin wondered how Coretta would accept his new responsibility. He needn't have worried. "I'm on your side," she assured him. Martin's obligations were growing at home as well as in the community. His first child, Yolanda Denise (Yoki), was two weeks old.

Martin drove slowly into the area where the mass meeting was to take place. Police cars circled the church and hundreds of people milled about, unable to get inside because the church was already filled to capacity. It took Martin 15 minutes to find a place to park his car.

Afraid that he was late, he hurried toward the church. Four thousand people were standing outside when he arrived. He could hear the voices of men, women, and children whispering, "Here he comes. Here comes King." Then over the top of the crowd, through a loudspeaker, he could hear the people inside singing "Onward Christian soldiers, marching as to war..."

The church was packed, and when he entered the sanctuary, a wild cheer went up. When Rosa Parks told her story, the crowd murmured, cheered, and called, "God bless you, sister."

Then Martin Luther King, Jr., stepped to the podium. His voice was clear and intense. He spoke from his heart.

> There comes a time when people get tired of being trampled over by the iron feet of oppression. There comes a time when people get tired of being flung across the abyss of humiliation where they experience the bleakness of nagging despair. There comes a time when people get tired of being pushed out of the glittering sunlight of life's July, and are left standing amidst the piercing chill of an alpine November. Now let us say that we are not here advocating violence. I want it to be known throughout this nation that we are Christian people.

Martin wanted to make it clear that the black people of Montgomery would not behave like the Ku Klux Klan.

In our protest there will be no cross burnings. No white person will be taken from his home by a hooded Negro mob and brutally murdered. There will be no threats or intimidation. We will be guided by the highest principles of law and order. Our actions must be guided by the deepest principles of our Christian faith. Love must be our regulating ideal!

When Martin finished speaking, the people, both inside and outside, cheered. They waved their hands, stamped their feet, and thanked God. When the thunderous applause subsided, Ralph Abernathy stepped forward, read their requirements to end the boycott, and asked all those in favor to stand. Every person in the hall stood, calling "Yes. Yes, brother. Amen." They agreed to stay off the buses until all of their demands were met. The civil rights movement had been launched, and Martin Luther King, Jr., had become its leader.

A young girl flags down a car. Car pools helped black people get around during the bus boycott, which lasted more than a year.

❧ FOUR ❧

Leading the Boycott
1955-1956

"One of the great glories of democracy is the right
to protest for right."
—Martin Luther King, Jr.

With Martin Luther King heading the MIA, the transportation committee made plans to get approximately 17,000 daily bus riders back and forth to work, shops, doctor's appointments, or wherever they had to go. Black-owned taxi companies agreed not to charge more than the cost of a bus ride, 10 cents. At first, members of the white community thought that if they just showed a little patience and exerted a little intimidation, the black movement would fall apart. "I have an idea," Police Commissioner Clyde Sellers said. "We will order Negro taxi companies to charge the legal minimum fare of 45 cents per customer." With this new law, cheap fares would cease.

"They will not be able to afford taxis," he said. "They will ride the buses." But the black people of Montgomery showed their solidarity and continued the boycott.

King and other MIA leaders were working day and night to ensure the success of the boycott. A car pool was organized and run with amazing precision. Forty-eight dispatch stations and forty-two pickup stations were established. Volunteer drivers transported people, and many wealthy black people, who ordinarily did not ride the buses, volunteered their cars. Doctors, lawyers, and business owners put in long hours as drivers. Soon it became necessary to open an office with 10 persons working in it. The media carried news of the boycott across the country and throughout the world. Donations began to arrive from many areas of the United States and from Japan, India, England, and France. By March, $65,000 was in the treasury, and the MIA was able to purchase 15 station wagons for the car pool. They were affectionately called "rolling churches." But many black people continued to walk.

Black citizens conducted themselves with such dignity that they even gained the admiration of some whites. One woman wrote the newspaper: "One feels that history is being made in Montgomery these days, the most important in her career. It is hard to imagine a soul so dead, a heart so hard, a vision so blinded and provincial as not to be moved with admiration at the quiet dignity, discipline, and dedication with which the Negroes have conducted their boycott."

Although a few Montgomery whites were sympathetic (three were even helping with the car pool), most were angry and afraid. Eventually many of them became mean. They wondered what was happening to their society. They were used to telling black people what to do, where to sit, where to eat; and black people had always obeyed. With the success of the boycott, something changed. White people weren't just concerned about losing seats on a bus. They sensed that they were losing their power, and that scared them. While the black people were sticking to their promise of nonviolence, white people were becoming more agitated. They were not prepared for the determination of the black community.

The White Citizens Council came up with an idea. "We'll take away the licenses of all car-pool drivers and we'll cancel their insurance," they said. "Without licenses and insurance they won't be able to drive."

The police department harassed and arrested drivers who gave rides to people. They gave tickets for blocking traffic, speeding, loitering, and for every imaginable reason.

One gloomy evening in January, Martin was driving home when two policemen on motorcycles came up beside him. "Pull over," one of the officers called.

Martin knew this was another white man's trick, but he had no choice. He braked the car and stopped at the side of the road.

A policeman leaned into the window. "You're under arrest."

"May I ask what for?"

The policeman looked at him. "Speeding," he said.

Martin and the two policemen stood at the side of the road, uncomfortably eyeing each other until a patrol car came.

"Okay. Inside." A uniformed officer from the patrol car held the door open and pointed a thumb to the back seat.

Sitting behind the policemen, Martin was scared. They weren't going toward town. They were headed in the opposite direction. They were moving into Klan country, where men were often beaten or hanged without anyone knowing what had happened to them. Martin could feel beads of perspiration forming on his forehead. "In the name of God," he whispered under his breath. "In the name of God . . ."

The driver turned onto a dark street that headed down under a bridge. Martin could feel his heart pounding. Were these

*King was arrested by
Montgomery police
during the bus boycott.*

really policemen? Were they going to kill him? He was trembling when he saw a sign on the horizon: Montgomery Jail.

Martin was relieved, but it was the first time he had been locked behind bars. He later recalled, "Strange gusts of emotion swept through me like cold winds."

News of his arrest spread quickly, and an angry crowd gathered in front of the jail. The police didn't want to let King go when Ralph Abernathy tried to post bond for his release. Outside, the crowd continued to grow, and inside, the police were getting nervous as they wondered what the crowd might do.

Before Abernathy returned, the police panicked. They decided that King could sign his own bond. "Turn King loose," they said. "Let the black devil go."

Although each incident made Martin Luther King stronger, some were worse than others because they were directed at his family. On January 30, Martin was speaking at a large meeting when he learned that his house had been bombed.

He jumped from the platform and hurried out the side door. By the time he reached home, more than 300 angry black people had already gathered. The men were armed with guns, clubs, rocks, and knives. "I ain't gonna move nowhere," a black man told a policeman.

King pushed his way through the angry mob to the front door. "Coretta! Coretta!"

"In here, Martin."

"You're safe? And Yoki?"

"She's fine." Then Coretta explained that when she heard a noise on the front porch, she had gone to the back of the house, where the baby was sleeping. When the bomb exploded, it sounded as though the whole front of the house had been blown away. Luckily, the bomb only split a pillar on the porch and shattered the front windows. The living room was filled with broken glass and smoke. Soon the house was filled with policemen and firemen. Mayor W. A. "Tacky" Gayle and the police commissioner were also there.

After talking with Coretta for a few minutes, Martin stepped out on the porch to face the shouting, cursing crowd, which was on the verge of violence. Montgomery could have been the scene of a fierce and bloody riot, but Martin Luther King showed the world what kind of man he was. He raised his arms and told the crowd:

> If you have weapons, take them home; if you do not have them, please do not seek them. We cannot solve this problem through violence. We must meet violence with nonviolence. Love your enemies, bless

them that curse you, pray for them that despitefully use you. Remember this movement will not stop, because God is with it.

These unforgettable words made Martin Luther King a living symbol. Although his house had just been badly damaged, and the lives of his wife and child had been threatened, he still preached love and forgiveness.

❦

On November 13, 1956, Dr. King was in court because of the city's order forbidding car pools. It was a sad day for King because he feared this order would mean the end of the boycott. Just then, Rex Thomas from the Associated Press (AP) news service handed him a slip of paper.

"Here is the decision you've been waiting for," Thomas said.

The AP wire read: "The United States Supreme Court to-day affirmed a decision of a special three-judge U.S. District Court in declaring Alabama's state and local laws requiring segregation on buses unconstitutional." Hearing this, a jubilant bystander cried, "God Almighty has spoken from Washington, D.C."

The news meant victory for the black people of Alabama and the beginning of change for both races. The following night, members of the Ku Klux Klan pulled their white hoods over their heads, and 40 carloads of them rode up and down the streets of Montgomery. Ordinarily, threats of Klan action were a signal for black people to stay in their homes, pull down the shades, and turn off the lights. This time, with new courage, they stood openly on porches as if they were watching a parade. Some of them dared to wave at the passing cars, and others just went about their business as if they didn't notice. After driving only a few blocks, the Klan cars disappeared back into the darkness from which they had come.

As the crowd cheered, Ralph Abernathy, left, *congratulated King,* front center, *after the Supreme Court decision. Coretta is between them.*

Before black people started riding buses under Alabama's new desegregation law, leaders (mostly ministers) in the black community organized training sessions at which they taught techniques of nonviolence. Leaders went into schools, where they urged students to accept the victory gracefully. "Don't brag," they said. "Don't boast." A flyer urged black people to accept their success with "a calm and loving dignity." It said: "If cursed, do not curse back. If struck, do not strike back, but evidence love and goodwill at all times. If another person is being molested, do not arise to go to his defense, but pray for the oppressor."

Unfortunately, no one undertook the responsibility of preparing citizens of the white community. The White Citizens Council threatened, "Any attempt to enforce this decision will lead to riots and bloodshed." On December 18, the city commissioners issued a statement that read in part, "The City Commission . . . will not yield one inch, but will do all in its power to oppose the integration of the Negro race with the white race in Montgomery. . . ."

The order for integration reached Montgomery on December 20, 1956. More than a year had passed since Rosa Parks had refused to give up her seat on the bus. Martin Luther King spoke to an overflow crowd at the evening's mass meeting. His voice resounded through the auditorium.

The White Citizens Council rallied against the court decision to desegregate buses.

Martin Luther King cautioned black people to accept their victory with dignity and to resist violence.

"This is the time that we must evince calm and wise restraint. Emotions must not run wild. Violence must not come from any one of us."

The following morning, December 21, more than a year after the boycott began, Dr. King, Ralph Abernathy, E. D. Nixon, and Reverend Glenn Smiley, a white minister, rode on Montgomery's first integrated bus.

At a meeting in Atlanta, the Southern Christian Leadership Conference was formed, and King was elected president.

Striding toward Freedom

1957-1958

*"Do your work so well that no one could do it better.
Do it so well that all the hosts of heaven and earth
will have to say: Here lived a man who did his job
as if God Almighty called him at this particular
time in history to do it."*
—Martin Luther King, Jr.

Integrating the buses had not been easy. It was a big achievement, but it solved only a small part of a much larger problem: the refusal of the white community to change its thinking and customs. Deeply ingrained in the hearts of white people, especially in the South, was the notion that black people came to this country to serve. White people thought that black people were inferior. They thought black people should be slaves and white people should be their masters.

The whole country had been watching Montgomery during the boycott, and black people in other southern states began talking about what could be done where they lived. On January 9, 1957, Martin Luther King and Ralph Abernathy drove to Atlanta to meet with black leaders from other southern states. During their meeting, 60 black ministers formed the Southern Leadership Conference on Transportation and

Non-Violent Integration, later to become the Southern Christian Leadership Conference (SCLC).

The meeting was cut short because violence erupted once again. The Ku Klux Klan and the White Citizens Council reacted violently to integrated buses. A black teenage girl was dragged from her home and beaten, a pregnant black woman was shot in the leg, and there was an outbreak of bombings. Ralph Abernathy's house was bombed and Dr. King found a bundle of smoldering dynamite on his front porch one night. To this he said, "Tell Montgomery that they can keep shooting and I'm going to stand up to them. Tell Montgomery that they can keep bombing and I'm going to stand up to them. If I had to die tomorrow morning I could die happy because I've been to the mountaintop and I've seen the Promised Land, and it's going to be here in Montgomery."

Bus service was stopped for a while, but the city officials and the business community finally asserted their authority. Rewards were offered and seven white men were arrested. Although the white jury found them not guilty, despite signed confessions, an important precedent had been established. White people had been caught and tried for crimes against black people. Terrorism in Montgomery declined, and bus service resumed. King triumphantly declared that, "A new Negro has been born in the South." With the success of the boycott, he was thrust into prominence, and he became a national leader. When he appeared in crowds, his followers shouted, "God bless you, Dr. King." In their prayers, they quietly gave thanks for the man who was bringing them freedom.

Martin Luther King was elected president of the SCLC at a February 14 meeting in New Orleans. The SCLC wanted to create a grass-roots freedom movement in the South, a movement that would involve all southern black people at a

Members of the Ku Klux Klan, who wear hoods and robes to conceal their identities, reacted violently to integration.

King addressed the crowd at the Prayer Pilgrimage in Washington.

local level. At the New Orleans meeting, black leaders asked President Dwight D. Eisenhower to call a White House conference on civil rights, but their request was refused.

In response, they planned a Prayer Pilgrimage for May 17, 1957, in Washington, D.C. The march drew so much attention that hundreds of white students, teachers, and professional people joined it. Movie stars from Hollywood, famous singers, and distinguished senators were there. They marched down the Mall (a large courtyard surrounded by government buildings) singing "The Battle Hymn of the Republic" and carrying signs that said: WE SEEK THE FREEDOM PROMISED IN 1865! NO U.S. DOUGH TO HELP JIM CROW! A CENTURY-OLD DEBT TO PAY!

The huge crowd circled the Lincoln Memorial. Some of the marchers lay down on the grass, took off their shoes, and unpacked picnic lunches. A newspaper reporter wrote:

Crowds welcomed King's important message: "Give us the ballot!"

Tens of thousands of petitioning Negroes had never been to Washington before, and probably would never come again. And now here they were. And this was their Washington, their very own capital, and this was their lawn and that great marble memorial was the memorial to the man who had emancipated them.

Dr. King had something important to say. The responsibility he felt for this moment weighed heavily on him as he stood before the marble statue of Abraham Lincoln, the man who had proclaimed freedom for black slaves. The crowd grew quiet, and King began to speak. "Give us the ballot!" his voice boomed over loudspeakers.

Give us the ballot and we will no longer have to worry the federal government about our basic rights. . . . Give us the ballot and we will fill the legislature with men of goodwill. Give us the ballot and we will get the people judges who love mercy....

The crowd communicated its approval by clapping, shouting, and roaring "amens." This was Martin Luther King's first truly national address.

Soon after the Prayer Pilgrimage, King was awarded the NAACP's (National Association for the Advancement of Colored People) Spingarn Medal for his contribution to race relations. He was the youngest recipient to receive that honor. Howard University, the Theological Seminary of the University of Chicago, and Morehouse College presented him with honorary degrees.

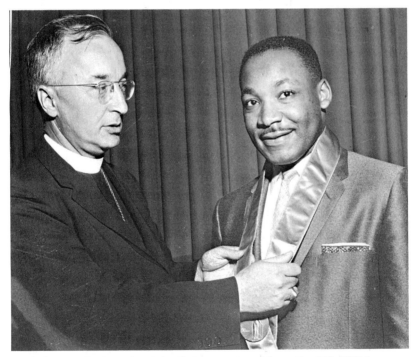

In 1957, King received the Spingarn award from the NAACP for his contribution to race relations.

Although Martin spent a great deal of time traveling to give speeches and attend meetings, he did get home in October when Martin Luther King III (Little Marty) was born. One night while he was home, Coretta noticed Martin making notes of the day's events.

"What are you doing up so late?" she asked.

"I'm writing a book," he told her. "It's about the bus boycott. I'm calling it *Stride toward Freedom.*"

At a meeting with Vice-President Richard M. Nixon on June 13, 1957, Martin Luther King and Ralph Abernathy helped arrange a White House conference for the following year.

The following September, a civil rights bill was passed by Congress, the first of its kind since 1875. The bill created the Civil Rights Commission. Although it was not a strong bill, it did indicate that the legislative branch of government was beginning to show some interest in civil rights.

Early in 1958, Dr. King turned his attention to the Crusade for Citizenship, which was the practical result of the Prayer Pilgrimage. The Crusade, which began on Lincoln's birthday with 20 large meetings across the country, was designed to register 5 million southern black voters by 1960. When King spoke in Miami, Florida, he told his followers, "Let us make our intentions clear. We must and we will be free. We want our freedom now. We want the right to vote now. We do not want freedom fed to us on a teaspoon. Under God we were born free. Misguided men robbed us of our freedom. We want it back." Then he said, "Remember the words of Jesus. 'He who lives by the sword will perish by the sword.' We must meet our white brothers with love."

On June 23, 1958, Martin Luther King, Jr., and three other civil rights leaders met with President Dwight

Eisenhower. A. Philip Randolph served as spokesman and read a six-page statement describing what black people wanted. The group made it clear that the black population was unhappy that the administration had not done more on its behalf.

King had hoped that Eisenhower would take a strong stand and push for legislation that would help black people. Once again he was disappointed.

On September 3, Martin and Coretta accompanied Ralph Abernathy to a Montgomery courtroom, where he was to testify against a man who had assaulted him. At the courtroom door, a guard refused to let Martin enter the room. When he asked if he could speak with Abernathy's lawyer, the officer snarled, "Boy, if you don't get out of here, you'll need a lawyer yourself." At that point, Martin was seized by two guards who twisted his arm into a hammerlock and led him to the police station.

When Coretta ran toward her husband, a guard stepped in front of her. "You want to go too, gal? Just nod your head." Martin called, "Don't say anything, darling."

King posted bond and was released. In court a few days later, a judge found him guilty of loitering and failing to obey an officer. The fine was $10 or 14 days in jail. King chose to go to jail. When Police Commissioner Sellers heard of the sentence, he paid the fine himself. He was furious. "You fools," he stormed. "King went to jail for publicity. Don't let him get away with it. Turn him loose."

❧

A short time later, Martin Luther King's first book was published, and he made public appearances across the country. One day while he was autographing books in a Harlem department store, an emotionally disturbed black woman pushed her way through the crowd and stood near him. "Are you Mr. King?" she asked.

"I am."

"Luther King," she cried, "I've been after you for five years." Then she took a sharp letter opener from beneath her dress and thrust it into his chest.

Martin was rushed to the hospital, where surgeons removed one of his ribs and part of his breastbone. The doctor told him, "If you had sneezed you would have drowned in your own blood."

News of King's stabbing flashed across the country. Radio and television stations broadcast hourly bulletins about his condition. Telegrams of sympathy came from the president and heads of state, but one letter did not come from a famous person. It was a letter that Martin would never forget.

Dear Dr. King,

I am a ninth grade student at the White Plains High School. While it shouldn't matter, I would like to mention that I am a white girl. I read in the paper of your misfortune and of your suffering. And I read that if you sneezed you would have died. I'm simply writing you to say that I'm glad you didn't sneeze.

Martin Luther King pleaded with people to practice the concepts of nonviolence during their struggle for civil rights. He won respect throughout the world for his courageous leadership.

∽ SIX ∽

We Shall Overcome
1959-1962

"It is a time for all America to end Jim Crow now."
—Martin Luther King, Jr.

In the weeks that followed his near-fatal stabbing, Martin had time to rest and spend some time alone. He thought about his work, his goals, and his philosophy of nonviolence. He wondered how Mohandas Gandhi's ideas related to civil rights problems in the United States. When his doctors thought he was well enough to leave the hospital, they released him, but warned him to take it easy until he regained his strength. Martin listened to his physicians and took advantage of this time to do something different.

The Kings decided to go to India. A year earlier Martin had received an invitation from the Gandhi Peace Foundation to visit India and learn more about nonviolent concepts and tactics. This was a perfect time to accept the invitation.

Martin and Coretta spent a month touring India. Martin spoke to large audiences, and he learned more about Gandhi

In 1959, the Kings moved from Montgomery, Alabama, to Atlanta, Georgia, and Martin preached at Ebenezer Baptist Church.

from Indian leaders and teachers. As Martin observed the people's faithfulness to Gandhi's teaching, his commitment to nonviolence was strengthened. Martin and Coretta returned to the United States on March 10, 1959. The trip had provided a unique spiritual experience and now Martin was ready to take his beliefs one step further. During the bus boycott, protesters had simply refrained from doing something—riding the bus. They had not broken any laws. The bus boycott was an example of passive resistance. After his trip to India, Martin began to think that sometimes it was necessary to refuse to obey some laws, to practice civil disobedience.

In November 1959, the Kings moved from Montgomery, Alabama, to Atlanta, Georgia, where the SCLC headquarters was located. There Martin joined his father as assistant pastor at Ebenezer Baptist Church.

Martin liked to spend time with his children. Three of them are pictured here: Bernice, upper left, *Martin Luther King III,* upper right, and *Yolanda,* lower right

Although Martin traveled often, the King family enjoyed being together, especially for dinner.

Martin's melodious voice rang from the pulpit. "I can't stop now. History has thrust something upon me which I cannot turn away. We must train our youth and adult leaders in the techniques of social change through nonviolent resistance. We must employ new methods of struggle. . . ." Martin's words were changing the thinking of black people. Little by little and day by day, they were learning to stand up bravely against a cruel and unjust tradition.

During the same period, James Lawson, a minister from Nashville, Tennessee, held workshops at which he taught the techniques of nonviolence. He also wrote a pamphlet on how it should be practiced. "Nonviolence," the brochure explained,

is a way of overcoming injustice, not of retaliating for it. Basically it is rooted in the recognition that your opponent is human. Being human, he will probably react with fear if you threaten him, but in the long run he is likely to respond with good will if you go out of your way to encourage it. . . . Gradually, if you hold fast to your nonviolent program, your opponent will gain respect for you. If your campaign succeeds, it will not be by defeating him but by removing his hostility.

On January 31, 1960, Joseph McNeill, a black student from North Carolina Agricultural and Technical College, entered a Woolworth's store and sat at its lunch counter. The waiter looked at him and said, "We don't serve Negroes." McNeill left quietly, but on his way home, his heart pounded and his anger grew. Sitting on the edge of his bed, he told the story to his roommate. They talked until late at night, each of them telling the other about past suffering, each believing that Martin Luther King was right. They felt that something had to be done. His roommate suggested that they go back the next day.

Gathering their courage and promising themselves to hold only a quiet demonstration, they walked into the store, across the lunchroom, and sat at the counter. The waiter glared at them. "I told you," he said. "We don't serve niggers."

McNeill and his roommate remained at the counter all day. The following morning two more students joined them. Within two weeks, many students in North Carolina heard about the sit-ins, and they also began to demand service in white restaurants. Three months later, nonviolent sit-ins had spread to more than 50 southern cities.

In Nashville, Jim Lawson and about 500 students from Fisk University marched to different lunch counters, often singing "We Shall Overcome," a song that became the anthem

These four young men (Joseph McNeill, far left) demanded service at a white lunch counter. Sit-ins soon spread across the South.

of the civil rights movement. The protesters were polite and well behaved, and they practiced Martin Luther King's ideas about nonviolence. They had a list of dos and don'ts. The list included things such as "Don't talk back. Sit up straight. Don't lash out. Don't hit back...." One of the students said, "We were dressed like we were going to church or out on a very special date or something. The young ladies wore long stockings and high heels. The guys put on ties and coats. We went there and sat all day. If someone had to leave to go to class, another person would sit in for him." Sometimes people called them names, poured ketchup or mustard on the students, or pushed them off the stools they were sitting on. Often they were arrested. But no matter what happened, the protesters remained nonviolent.

While the sit-ins were gaining momentum across the

South, the King family continued to grow. On January 30, 1961, the Kings' third child, Dexter Scott, was born.

John F. Kennedy had become the new president of the United States 10 days earlier. At first, the results of the election gave new hope to the civil rights movement, but King soon felt that Kennedy did not fully understand the evils and the extent of segregation. With or without help from Washington, however, the movement would go on. King and his associates were not about to stop what they had started.

In March, a new campaign was initiated. The students who had been participating in sit-ins decided to test a Supreme Court decision. The Court had ruled that segregation in all areas of public transportation was illegal.

"We will get on buses," they said, "and ride through the South. People will see that integration has not happened— that the Supreme Court decision has been ignored. We'll make white leaders face up to the fact that segregation is still alive." The college students and others who rode these buses became known as "Freedom Riders." They wanted to let the whole world know that the law was being broken in the South when black people had to stand in "colored" waiting rooms in bus stations. They still weren't allowed to eat in "white" restaurants in the South, and restrooms were still labeled COLORED MEN, WHITE MEN, COLORED WOMEN, WHITE WOMEN.

King was in Washington on May 4 when the first riders climbed aboard the buses, one a Trailways bus and the other a Greyhound bus. He shook their hands and gave them hugs. "God be with you," he said. As the buses pulled away from the curb, he wondered what would happen to the brave young people.

The buses rolled down the highway, traveling safely

In Anniston, Alabama, an angry mob threw a bomb inside one of the buses used by the Freedom Riders. Many riders were injured.

through Virginia. But in South Carolina they met trouble. The buses stopped at Rockhill, where the riders got off and walked into a "white" waiting room. There, a group of angry men attacked them and knocked them to the floor. The riders looked to the police, who were standing nearby, for help, but the police just stood with their arms folded.

Although the Freedom Riders were injured and bleeding, their spirits were not broken. "We will not give up," they told one another as they stumbled back on the bus. And they did not give up. The South was exploding with a new energy.

On Mother's Day, May 14, the two buses carrying the Freedom Riders arrived in Alabama. Just outside Anniston, an armed mob surrounded the first bus. The mob smashed windows, punctured tires, and tossed a fire bomb inside. As

When the Freedom Riders reached Montgomery, Alabama, an armed crowd attacked them. James Zwerg (above), a student at the University of Wisconsin, was beaten until he was unconscious.

the driver and the Freedom Riders tried to escape from the burning bus, many were attacked and beaten. The second bus raced on to Birmingham, Alabama, where a gang of local toughs was waiting. The Freedom Riders were assaulted and two of them, James Person, a black man, and James Peck, a white man, were brutally beaten while the police watched. Peck's face required 53 stitches. He was called a "nigger lover." Both bus drivers quit their jobs. Because the bus companies feared further damage to their property, they refused to allow their buses to continue to Montgomery. The riders had to abandon their plan and fly out of the city.

However, a second group of Freedom Riders boarded a bus in Nashville, Tennessee, and headed for Montgomery, Alabama, so the symbolic journey could continue. They were singing "We Shall Overcome" as the bus crept slowly down the quiet streets of Montgomery. There were no crowds, no patrol cars, no police. But when the bus pulled into the terminal, a crowd of several hundred angry white people was there to meet them. The crowd was armed with baseball bats, iron pipes, chains—all sorts of weapons. Both white and black Freedom Riders were attacked. Voices from the crowd shouted, "Kill the nigger lovers." James Zwerg, a white student from Wisconsin, and John Seigenthaler, who was sent by President Kennedy to observe the situation, were beaten until they were unconscious. The violence continued for about 20 minutes before the police appeared, but no arrests were made. When a reporter asked Police Commissioner L.B. Sullivan if he had called for an ambulance, Sullivan said, "No. Every white ambulance in town reports their vehicles have broken down."

King was in Atlanta when he saw the ugly scene on television. He decided to fly to Montgomery. The following evening, he spoke at a mass meeting at Ralph Abernathy's First Baptist Church. Twelve hundred black people and a few white people packed the church while a white mob gathered outside. The crowd grew until 3,000 to 4,000 angry white people surrounded the building. They burned a car and threw rocks and bottles through the windows. Inside the church, a baritone voice calmly sang, "Leaning on His Everlasting Arms."

Afraid of what might happen next, King hurried to the basement and telephoned Robert Kennedy, the U.S. attorney general. After hearing what King had to say, Kennedy told him, "Federal marshals are on the way." Six hundred federal marshals, who had been assembling at a nearby air base, arrived on the scene, but there were not enough of them to control the crowd. Attorney General Kennedy telephoned the governor of Alabama, John Patterson, and told him he had a choice. Either he could provide protection for the people inside the church, or President Kennedy would federalize the National Guard and take care of the problem himself. The governor called out about 300 troops, and the federal marshals tossed tear gas bombs into the disorderly mob. It was late that night when the crowd finally went home. People inside the church joined hands and sang.

Robert Kennedy asked the Freedom Riders to slow down their campaign to allow time for a cooling-off period, but they scoffed at his request. "We've been cooling off for one hundred years," they said. "If we got any cooler we'd be in a deep freeze."

Things did not cool off. Once again Martin Luther King sat in horror before the television set, this time watching news clips of the crisis that was triggered when James Meredith sought admission to the University of Mississippi.

When King saw the violence that greeted the Freedom Riders in Montgomery, he flew there to speak at a mass meeting.

A black air force veteran, Meredith tried to register as a student. Federal marshals had come to help him, but Governor Ross Barnett and a group of state troopers turned them away. In front of the administration building, white students paraded back and forth singing "Glory, glory, segregation" to the tune of "The Battle Hymn of the Republic."

Later, when the federal officers again tried to let Meredith register, a battle broke out, and the white people opened fire. Two people were killed, and three hundred seventy-five were injured. Meredith was finally admitted to the university, but he had to be escorted to his classes by federal marshals.

The country learned that beatings, bombings, humiliation, and fire would not stop the civil rights movement. "We will wear them down," King said. "We will wear them down with our ability to suffer."

"We will wear them down with our ability to suffer."
— Martin Luther King, Jr.

In Birmingham, Alabama, Martin Luther King was arrested and locked in a dark cell by himself.

SEVEN

The Battle for Freedom

1963-1964

*"It was our faith that as Birmingham goes,
so goes the South."*
—Martin Luther King, Jr.

Spirits ran high in black communities in the South. Black people's battle cry was "Free by '63," and Birmingham, Alabama, became the next battleground in the fight for civil rights.

As in Montgomery, demonstrators once again had to participate in training sessions, and each participant was required to sign a commitment card that read:

I hereby pledge myself—my person and my body— to the nonviolent movement. Therefore I will keep the following ten commandments:

1. Meditate daily on the teachings and life of Jesus.
2. Remember that the nonviolent movement in Birmingham seeks justice and reconciliation— not victory.

3. Walk and talk in the manner of love, for God is love.
4. Pray daily to be used by God in order that all men might be free.
5. Sacrifice personal wishes in order that all men might be free.
6. Observe with both friend and foe the ordinary rules of courtesy.
7. Seek to perform regular service for others and for the world.
8. Refrain from the violence of fist, tongue, or heart.
9. Strive to be good in spiritual and bodily health.
10. Follow the directions of the movement and of the captains on a demonstration.

Careful training was needed because racism in Birmingham was even more extreme than in many other parts of the South. If Birmingham was to be integrated, King knew it would require the best kind of leadership, organization, and determination. He was intent. "We'll march, and we'll fill up the jails," he said. "... If enough people are willing to go to jail, I believe it will force the city officials to act or force the federal government to act."

∽

For the first few days, the demonstrations were unusual because of the false politeness of the police, under the command of Commissioner Eugene "Bull" Connor. Connor was a racist, and he was very effective at "keeping black people in their place," usually with violence. This time, however, the demonstrators were only asked to show parade permits for marching. When no permits were shown, the demonstrators were arrested.

After a few days, Bull Connor became impatient. He had hundreds of black people in the Birmingham jail, but more demonstrators kept arriving. Also, as the SCLC posted bail for those who were arrested, the former prisoners returned to march again. Connor was seeing the same faces over and over. To stop the marches, a judge issued an injunction, or order, that prohibited the SCLC, Martin Luther King, Jr., and the marchers from participating in demonstrations. But King decided that that was an unfair law, and the demonstrations continued.

On April 12, 1963, a bright, sunny day, King led 50 marchers downtown. As he turned around, they waved to him. They clapped their hands and sang as they moved closer and closer to the line of police that barricaded the street.

"Look around you," King said to Ralph Abernathy.

The police were everywhere—on foot, on motorcycles, in patrol cars, and standing on rooftops with guns silhouetted against the sky.

When King and Abernathy came face-to-face with Bull Connor, they knelt down in prayer.

"Take 'em!" Connor shouted.

The marchers were grabbed by the seats of their pants and thrown into police vans. Sirens howled as the vans sped toward the jail.

King was locked in a dark cell by himself. He was not allowed to use the telephone or see a lawyer. Coretta, who had given birth to Bernice Albertine on March 28, was worried about her husband's safety. A few days later, a lawyer finally came with bail money for the other demonstrators who had been arrested, but King remained in jail.

New recruits arrived in Birmingham. The demonstrators continued to march, get arrested, and get bailed out each day.

In spite of daily arrests, black people in Birmingham continued to demonstrate in order to gain their civil rights.

The Birmingham police arrested demonstrators and took them to jail in police vans. Other demonstrators took their places. The jails became full, and the police became more violent.

And each day the Birmingham police treated them more and more harshly. Making the situation even worse, newly elected Alabama Governor George Wallace set an example for radical racial behavior by openly defying federal law. Wallace preached, "Segregation now, segregation tomorrow, segregation forever!"

Finally, on Saturday, April 20, King was released on bail. The movement needed his leadership. It also needed a new strategy. Some of the leaders wanted to use children in the marches, but King felt uncertain about the idea. He didn't want children to get hurt.

"We must try," his supporters insisted. "Let us try."

On May 2, about 1,000 boys and girls gathered at the Sixteenth Street Baptist Church. It was "D" day, the beginning of an even more serious battle in Birmingham. Small groups of 10 to 50 children marched to the center of town. They came, wave upon wave, singing and clapping. Many were arrested. The police ran out of vans to transport them, and the jails were filled. The next day thousands more children and their parents assembled at the church.

As they marched, shouting "We want freedom," the firemen held heavy hoses, and policemen hung on to dogs that strained at their leashes. Commissioner Bull Connor yelled until the veins stuck out on his neck, "Go back to your church!" But the marchers kept moving forward.

"Let 'em have it!" Connor yelled as he signaled the firemen to turn on their hoses. Columns of water crashed into the children, knocking them down, ripping their clothes, shoving them against the sides of buildings, driving them, bleeding and crying, into a nearby park. Black bystanders, who had not been trained in the techniques of nonviolence, became angry and hurled bricks and bottles at the firemen.

Bull Connor, top, right, *ordered Birmingham firemen to turn their hoses on the young marchers. Some sought shelter in a doorway.*

At the command of Bull Connor, police dogs attacked the demonstrators. Pictures of the violence shocked the world.

Then the commissioner ordered the dogs to be unleashed. The animals charged, snarling and biting. The young marchers rolled on the ground as the dogs dug their teeth into the children's arms and legs. Torn and beaten, some of the marchers returned to the church. Hundreds of others went to jail.

Pictures of the violence were seen in newspapers and on television screens around the world. Birmingham became a scandal. King had public opinion on his side.

The demonstrations and Commissioner Connor's violent reaction to them continued until the following Tuesday. By then about 2,000 demonstrators were in jail. The police used school buses to transport those arrested to special holding pens because the jails were overflowing. After the demonstration on Tuesday, May 7, a group of white community leaders formed a committee to come to terms with the demands of the black community. The agreement, reached on Friday, May 10, called for desegregation of lunch counters, restrooms, fitting rooms, and drinking fountains within 90 days. White businesses promised to hire black people and upgrade their positions in stores and factories. They agreed to cooperate with lawyers who were working for the release of jailed protesters. They also pledged to set up a committee to help black people and white people communicate with each other.

On Saturday, the day after the agreement, some angry white people bombed the house of A. D. King, Martin's brother. They also bombed the Gaston Hotel, where Martin had stayed during the demonstrations. Enraged by the incidents, black people poured onto the streets. A policeman was stabbed, and taxis were overturned. Cars, stores, and two apartment houses were burned. By Sunday morning, peace had been restored, but Martin, who had gone home to Atlanta, returned to Birmingham to continue his appeal for nonviolence. In an

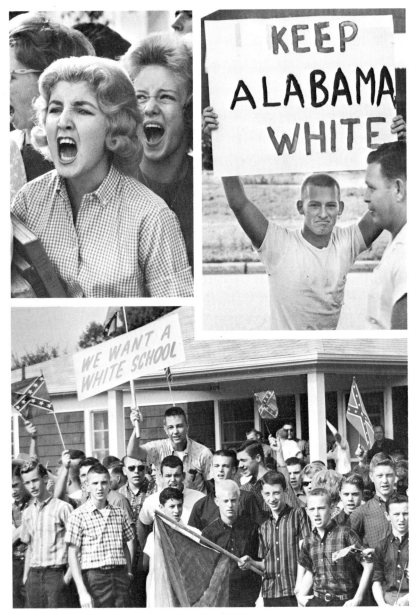

Angry white people in Alabama demonstrated against integration.
The Confederate flag, bottom photo, *symbolized their beliefs.*

Leaders of the March on Washington met with President Kennedy, fifth from the right. *King is* third from the left.

effort to reach the young men in the community, he set out on his "pool room pilgrimage." King and Abernathy went into bars and pool halls. They pleaded with young black men to adopt the attitude of nonviolence. Once again, King was successful. Many teenagers pulled knives from their belts and handed them to him. Others gave up their guns.

King told a gathering of 1,000 followers, "We will go on despite dogs and fire hoses. We will go on because we have started a fire in Birmingham that water cannot put out. We are going on because we love Birmingham and we love democracy. And we are going to remain nonviolent." And then he said, "Don't worry about your children who are in jail. The eyes of the world are upon them."

In June, the Kennedy administration requested that Congress pass new civil rights laws that would ensure equal

"I have a dream," King told the 250,000 people gathered for the March on Washington. His powerful words renewed people's hope.

justice and opportunity for all people in the United States. Fourteen important civic, religious, and labor organizations decided to plan a demonstration in Washington, D.C., to dramatize the issue. They thought the demonstration would help gain support from all over the country. The planners hoped that at least 100,000 people would participate.

On the morning of August 28, 250,000 people, both black and white, peacefully assembled for the historic March on Washington. The group marched from the Washington Monument to the Lincoln Memorial, where they listened to many speakers and entertainers. Martin Luther King, Jr., was the last person to speak on that hot, muggy day. People were wiping sweat from their foreheads. Their feet hurt, and they were tired of listening to speeches. But when King was introduced, the crowd burst into cheers and applause. Wearing a dark suit and feeling a bit nervous, he stepped to the podium. He looked out at the sea of people. Some were waving white handkerchiefs and calling out, "God bless you, brother." Finally, they became silent as he began his speech, one of the most memorable speeches of modern times.

"I have a dream today," he began.

I have a dream that one day on the red hills of Georgia, the sons of former slaves and the sons of former slave owners will be able to sit down together at the table of brotherhood. . . . I have a dream that my four little children will one day live in a nation where they will be judged not by the color of their skin, but by the content of their character. . . .

This is our hope. This is the faith I shall return to the South with. With this faith we will be able to hew out of the mountain of despair a stone of hope. With this faith we will be able to transform the jangling discords of our nation into a beautiful symphony of brotherhood. With this faith we will... stand up for freedom together, knowing that we will be free one day.

This will be the day when all of God's children will be able to sing with new meaning 'My country 'tis of thee, sweet land of liberty... from every mountainside let freedom ring....'

Let freedom ring.... Let it ring in every village and hamlet, from every state and every city, we will be able to join hands and sing in the words of the old Negro spiritual: 'Free at last! Free at last! Thank God Almighty, we're free at last!'

At the March on Washington, people peacefully demonstrated for equal justice and opportunity for members of all races.

Firemen remove the body of a black child from the Sixteenth Street Baptist Church in Birmingham, Alabama. She was one of four girls killed when a bomb was thrown through an open window while the children were attending Sunday school.

But freedom was yet to be won for many. Sunday, September 15, was also a hot day. In Birmingham, Alabama, as children attended their Sunday school classes at the Sixteenth Street Baptist Church, a package was thrown through one of the open windows. A few seconds later, the package, which contained sticks of dynamite, exploded. Four little girls were killed, and many more children were badly injured.

On November 22, 1963, President John Kennedy was assassinated while riding in a motorcade through Dallas, Texas. The nation, as well as the rest of the world, grieved. There were also threats on King's life. "I don't think I'm going to live until I reach 40," he told Coretta.

Martin Luther King was congratulated by King Olav V of Norway after receiving the Nobel Peace Prize.

When Kennedy was killed, Vice-President Lyndon B. Johnson became president. Congress, responding to the pressure of unrest and the influence of the new president— who was a southerner—passed the Civil Rights Act of 1964. On July 2, King and other black leaders, members of the president's cabinet, and J. Edgar Hoover (head of the Federal Bureau of Investigation, or FBI) were present when President Johnson signed the bill in the East Ballroom of the White House. Over national radio and television, Johnson said, "Those who are equal before God shall now be equal in the polling booths, classrooms, in the factories, and in hotels, restaurants, movie theaters, and other places that provide service to the public."

Even though the Civil Rights Act passed, King was discouraged with the slow progress of the movement. Suffering from exhaustion, he was in an Atlanta hospital on October 14 when he learned that he had won the Nobel Peace Prize. It is a prize awarded to people who have made valuable contributions to the good of humanity.

"For a while I thought it was a dream," he said. "Then I realized it was true."

Congratulations came from all over the world. Reporters swarmed into his hospital room to get their stories, but J. Edgar Hoover bellowed, "He is the last person in the world who should have received it." Hoover was one of the most powerful men in Washington. He intimidated presidents and legislators, and he was convinced that King was a Communist—an enemy.

Although black people had made great strides toward freedom, they still had a distance to go. They were not a free people. Not yet. King believed the next step was to ensure their right to vote. "There are still more Negroes in jail," he said, "than there are on the voting rolls."

In Selma, Alabama, people from many parts of the country joined the marches to gain voting rights for black people.

❧ EIGHT ☙

Crossing the Bridge
1965-1966

"I am not willing to kill, but I am willing to die."
—Martin Luther King, Jr.

If King's dream was going to become a reality and black people were going to gain the power of the ballot, then voter registration had to be the next step. So 1965 began with a campaign to register voters in Alabama's "Black Belt," an area heavily populated with black people. Plans were underway to move into Selma, where black people outnumbered white people but represented only 1 percent of the voters. Out of 15,000 black people, only 350 were registered to vote. When King began the Selma campaign at Brown's Chapel Methodist Church, he told 700 black people, "We are going to start a march on the ballot boxes by the thousands."

On January 18, hundreds of people marched to the courthouse to register and patiently stood outside. Sheriff Jim Clark met the group. He told John Lewis, a young black protester, "You are nothing but an agitator. You're the lowest form of humanity." Clark was a heavyset man, weighing about 220 pounds, and he was very effective at maintaining Selma's racist policies.

The marches during January and February resulted in hundreds of arrests. Waiting to register, black people stood for hours in front of the courthouse, while Sheriff Clark shouted at them through a bullhorn. Sometimes they were told that the office of the registrar was closed. Other times a few black people were allowed to fill out applications, but then the applications were crumpled up and tossed in the wastebasket. The clerk might say, "You made a mistake," or "Can't you read?" Sometimes black registrants were asked very difficult or confusing questions which they couldn't answer.

At the beginning of February, King and Abernathy again planned to lead several hundred marchers from Brown's Chapel to the courthouse. King felt tired as he stood before the protesters at a mass meeting, but his determination never weakened: "I come to tell you tonight that violence may win a temporary victory, but it cannot win permanent peace." He explained the purpose of the march. "For the past month, the Negro citizens of Selma, Alabama, and Dallas County, have been attempting to register by the hundreds. To date...none has received notice of successful registration....Now we must call a halt to these injustices."

The marchers had walked only three blocks when they were stopped by Wilson Baker, the new director of the city police. Baker disliked excessive brutality, but he was willing to use it in some situations. "This is a direct attempt to violate the city's parade ordinance," he said. "You will have to break up into small groups."

King disagreed. "We don't feel we are disobeying any law," he replied. "We feel we have the constitutional right to

King addressed a group of demonstrators who wanted to register to vote in Selma, Alabama. His determination never weakened.

walk down to the courthouse."

"You are wrong," Baker said, and he had all of them arrested. The arrest of the Nobel Prize winner made headlines in newspapers around the world.

On February 10, when a group of 165 children gathered to protest, Sheriff Clark and his deputies, in their trucks and cars, encircled the children. They used clubs and electric prods (long, pointed instruments that give an electric shock) to force the children out of town like cattle.

∽

A week later, during a demonstration in Marion, Alabama, 30 miles (48 kilometers) from Selma, Jimmie Lee Jackson, a young pulpwood cutter, was killed by state troopers. Many people throughout the country were outraged. King wanted to direct these strong feelings into some positive action. He organized a march from Selma to Montgomery, the capital of Alabama. The people wanted to bring their case to Governor

King, left, *wanted equality for all people. Alabama Governor
George Wallace,* right, *preached, "Segregation forever!"*

George Wallace, the segregationist leader of the state, but
Wallace issued an order prohibiting the march.

On Sunday, March 7, about 600 protesters, equipped with
food, bedrolls, and blankets for the 54-mile (87-kilometer)
trip, met at Brown's Chapel. As the demonstrators began
their march, troopers, who were waiting on the Edmund
Pettus Bridge, got into position and pulled on gas masks.
Because King was at his home in Atlanta, Georgia, Hosea
Williams of the SCLC and John Lewis of the SNCC (Student
Nonviolent Coordinating Committee) led the march. When
the marchers crossed the bridge, the state troopers gave them
three minutes to turn around. Crowds of local white citizens
were taunting the marchers from the outskirts. Williams asked
the troopers, "May we have a word with you?"

"There's not going to be any talking today," an officer
shouted through a bullhorn.

When the marchers did not turn back, the order was given: "Troopers, forward!" The state police advanced, throwing cannisters of tear gas and beating the marchers with nightsticks and bull whips. Troopers rode their horses over fallen bodies. They swung at men, women, and children as they passed. One trooper whipped a marcher across the back and shouted, "March nigger! You wanted to march! I'm gonna help you." The white onlookers cheered. One yelled, "Kill them." When the attack was over, John Lewis had a fractured skull and many others were seriously injured.

That night, television news of the event shook the nation. It was called "Bloody Sunday." Newspapers all over the world made Selma famous, and people everywhere were shocked. Martin was deeply moved by the tragedy.

After "Bloody Sunday," King announced that he would lead a march from Selma to Montgomery on March 9. "I am asking American clergymen—black and white—to join us in Selma."

On "Bloody Sunday," state troopers, wearing gas masks, beat and teargassed demonstrators as white onlookers cheered.

State troopers blocked the road so the marchers could not pass.

An injunction was issued to prevent the march, and President Johnson asked King to postpone it. Johnson even sent the U.S. attorney general to Selma to intervene. Finally an agreement was reached. If the marchers turned back after crossing the bridge, there would be no violence. If they continued toward Montgomery, the troopers would "enforce the law" as they had done before.

Fifteen hundred demonstrators walked the same path from Brown's Chapel to the bridge, but this time there was no bloodshed. After crossing the bridge, King led the group in prayer, then told them to turn around.

∽

One of the demonstrators was Reverend James Reeb, a white Unitarian minister from Boston. He had told a friend, "It is time for those who care for human freedom to make a

After crossing the Edmund Pettus Bridge, King led the demonstrators in prayer.

direct witness." Leaving his wife and four children safely behind in Boston, he traveled to Selma to participate in the march.

After the march, Reeb and a few other white ministers dined at a cafe owned by black people. They ate soul food (fried chicken, collard greens, corn bread, and sweet-potato pie), then left the restaurant. As they passed a cafe called the Silver Moon, a voice called, "Hey, you want to know what it's like to be a real nigger?" Four white youths came out from the shadows and beat the ministers with clubs. Reeb's skull was crushed and he lapsed into a coma. An ambulance sped him to a hospital in Birmingham, where he died two days later.

Reeb's murder provoked a storm of indignation. The day after the attack, 70 priests and nuns from Chicago arrived in Selma to protest the slaying. In Washington, President Johnson took a strong stand on the black cause when he addressed a joint session of Congress. While Johnson spoke, Martin Luther King sat alone in the living room of a friend and cried.

"I speak tonight for the dignity of man," the president said, "and I speak for the destiny of democracy. . . . What happened in Selma is part of a far larger movement which reaches into every section and state of America. It is the effort of American Negroes to secure for themselves the full blessings of American life. Their cause must be our cause too . . . ." He was interrupted by applause many times, but he continued.

"And we *shall* overcome!"

In the meantime, a federal judge ruled that the protesters had a constitutional right to march from Selma to Montgomery. Governor Wallace, who was opposed to the march, said he could not guarantee their protection. Nevertheless, the five-day march finally began on March 21. More than 3,000 demonstrators crossed the Edmund Pettus Bridge. As they passed, singing "We Shall Overcome," Sheriff Clark stood by quietly. He wore a button that expressed his feeling. It said "Never."

Days later, just outside Montgomery, over 20,000 people joined the march, which ended with a rally on the steps of the Alabama State Capitol.

Influenced by the protesters' efforts and the dramatic march, Congress passed the Voting Rights Act. On August 6, 1965, when President Johnson signed it into law, both Martin Luther King, Jr., and Rosa Parks were present. The new law abolished poll taxes (a tax that had to be paid in order to vote), literacy tests, and other requirements that had been used to disqualify black people when they tried to register to

The demonstrators finally marched from Selma to Montgomery, where troopers barred their entry to the state capitol.

President Johnson talked with King about the Voting Rights Act.

vote. Federal examiners were sent into Black Belt counties to register black voters.

During this same period, Martin was also trying to organize cities outside the South to use nonviolent techniques. Among other places, he traveled to New York, Boston, and Chicago. He led 18,000 people to the Boston Common during a heavy rain and then gave a 40-minute speech on racial injustice.

Martin discovered that the North was much harder to organize than the South. There were no signs that said BLACKS ONLY or WHITES ONLY, but racial discrimination was everywhere. Segregation was not part of the law, but in practice such treatment was common. Black people were only hired for certain jobs, mainly low-paying ones. Frequently, in black neighborhoods, city services such as housing inspection and garbage collection were inadequate. Parks and recreation centers were poorly maintained and did not compare favorably with those supplied for the white population. Street repairs were done carelessly, and sometimes they weren't done at all.

Many black people in the North supported the ideas of the militant Black Power movement, a group that thought nonviolent methods were too slow in getting results. They rejected white values and did not believe white people were sincere in their support for the rights of black people. Black Power leaders urged black people to gain control of their own communities and form their own standards. Riots took place in several cities.

Although King made some progress in the North, he wasn't as effective there as he had been in the South. In many cases, the church played a smaller role in the lives of northern blacks. The populations in many northern cities were larger, and the problems of the black people there differed from those of their southern counterparts.

King rented a run-down apartment in Lawndale, a black ghetto on the West Side of Chicago. In July 1965, he led 30,000 people in a march to City Hall to protest segregation in Chicago's public schools. Northern schools didn't "officially" keep black children out of white schools, but black people were not welcome to live anywhere except in black neighborhoods. Where a child lived determined which school he or she attended, so schools were automatically segregated.

King made speeches and led nonviolent marches and rallies to dramatize the inequality of the system and force change. Earlier, in Atlanta, he had begun Operation Breadbasket, an effort to get businesses to hire black people. He tried the same thing in Chicago, and he also organized tenants' unions to force landlords to repair their buildings.

Many landlords owned ghetto buildings that were dangerous for people to live in. They were overcrowded. Often,

King, left, *and* Abernathy, right, *were stoned during a march in Cicero, Illinois.*

five or six children lived with their parents in two rooms. Plaster fell from the walls and ceilings. Rats crawled in through holes in walls and around pipes. Sometimes the plumbing didn't work, and sometimes there wasn't any heat or hot water. Landlords charged high rents for these dilapidated apartments but wouldn't make repairs. The tenants' unions held rent strikes to force landlords to fix the buildings. Tenants refused to pay rent until repairs were made. Although rent strikes worked for a few thousand people, hundreds of thousands more needed to be organized, and that took time. Many black people in Chicago were impatient. Others felt powerless. They could vote, ride buses, eat at lunch counters, and share waiting rooms, bathrooms, and drinking fountains,

James Meredith was the first black person to enroll at the University of Mississippi.

but they couldn't change their living conditions. Black people were tired of living in the worst apartments, having the lowest-paying jobs, and sending their children to the worst schools. They were tired of waiting and tired of nonviolence.

In July, their frustration reached a peak. During a very hot day, some children tried to stay cool by playing in the water from a fire hydrant. But opening a fire hydrant was illegal, so the police came to close it and send the children home. Since there were no swimming pools in the area, many people thought the police action was unfair. One thing quickly led to another, and a three-day riot erupted. A terrible riot had already occurred in Watts, a black area of Los Angeles. A riot in Cleveland followed the one in Chicago.

A month before the Chicago riot, in June 1966, James Meredith, the young black man who had enrolled at the

University of Mississippi, decided to find out if freedom had really come to that state. He planned to walk from Memphis, Tennessee, to Jackson, Mississippi. He wanted to make a private statement, without press or demonstrations. On the second day of the march, as he approached Hernando, Mississippi, a shotgun blast came from behind a tree. Meredith fell to the ground, his back peppered with buckshot.

King was holding a staff meeting in Atlanta when he heard the shocking news. He rushed to a telephone and dialed Memphis. He tried to be patient as he clutched the phone and hoped his worst fear was not true. Then came the good news: "Meredith is alive."

The next day King flew to Memphis, where he and other civil rights leaders sat by Meredith's bed and promised him that his efforts had not been in vain. "We will march for you," King told him. "We will call it the James Meredith March Against Fear."

Although it was a brave act, this march became a painful experience for King. As the marchers moved down the highway, militant young blacks joined them, shouting "No more nonviolence. We're not for nonviolence no more." King shuddered at the sound of their defiant voices. "We shall overrun" could be heard above other voices that were singing "We shall overcome."

The sun beat down on the tired marchers as they continued through the countryside and down village streets. In the blistering heat, perspiration ran down their bodies. Their clothes were damp. Their feet hurt. Their mouths were dry.

The march had several leaders besides Martin Luther King, and they did not all agree with each other about the philosophy of nonviolence. Like many black people, some of the leaders were becoming impatient. They wanted to hit

Stokely Carmichael, left, *shouted a new slogan: "Black Power."*

After Meredith was shot, King, front center, *led the James Meredith March Against Fear from Memphis, Tennessee, to Jackson, Mississippi.*

back when they were hit. One of these militant blacks was Stokely Carmichael, who objected to white people marching with the group. Against King's wishes, Carmichael began raising his fist and shouting a new slogan: "Black power!" King was horrified because he thought the slogan gave the impression of black supremacy, which he felt would be as evil as white supremacy.

As the march progressed, Carmichael and his followers became more hostile and noisy. The marchers paused in Philadelphia, Mississippi, where three civil rights workers had been murdered two years earlier. King conducted a memorial service for them. During the service, a crowd of white people encircled them and then attacked. The police looked the other way until some of the demonstrators started fighting back. Then the police moved in and broke up the fight. That night, at their campsite, the marchers were shot at, and some blacks who had guns shot back. King vowed to return to Philadelphia again in a nonviolent march.

When the demonstrators reached Canton, they attempted to set up camp on the grounds of an all-black elementary school. The police told them to leave, but King and other protesters refused to go. State police moved in, hurling grenades and tear gas while battering marchers with whips, sticks, and gun butts. Dr. King escaped injury when he jumped up on a truck.

The group eventually reached Jackson, Mississippi, and held a rally on the grounds of the State Capitol. About 15,000 people, including many famous entertainers, attended. Hundreds of National Guard soldiers with rifles stood around the grounds. The march had lasted from June 6 until June 26.

The demonstrators
marched to Phila-
delphia, Mississippi,
where they held a
memorial service for
three civil rights
workers who had been
murdered there.

At the Tomb of the Unknown Soldier, King joined other religious leaders in a demonstration against the Vietnam War.

✑ NINE ✑

Trouble in Memphis

1967-1968

"If a man has not found something worth giving
his life for, he is not fit to live."
—Martin Luther King, Jr.

By 1967, people were deeply and bitterly divided over
the United States' involvement in the Vietnam War. People
disagreed about whether U.S. troops should fight in Vietnam.
Martin Luther King, Jr., was very clear about where he stood
on nonviolence and on the war issue. He was against the
war, and his position made many people angry. They advised
him to stick to civil rights and not get involved in international
affairs. But he was against violence anywhere. He knew that
war was expensive. If the government spent lots of money on
the Vietnam War, it would have less money to spend on
programs to help the poor. He said, "I'm not going to sit by
and see war escalated without saying anything about it. It is
worthless to talk about integrating if there is no world to
integrate in." The people who believed U.S. troops should
stay in Vietnam also felt strongly about the war. Both sides

Throughout the country, King spoke for peace and civil rights.

thought they were right, and the general mood of the nation was one of anger.

In the early spring of 1967, Martin's book, *Where Do We Go from Here: Chaos or Community?* was published. On February 25, he gave his first speech devoted entirely to Vietnam. He said the war was "one of history's most cruel and senseless wars." He spoke from his heart and felt a deep sadness for the country when he called it "our tragedy. . . ." He also said, "It is our guilt."

More speeches followed in Chicago, Illinois, and Berkeley, California. On April 15, more than 125,000 New Yorkers demonstrated against the war by marching from Central Park to the United Nations Plaza Building.

Although King was actively protesting the war, he continued to speak in support of the civil rights movement. Black militants also spoke out. The following July, black communities in Newark, New Jersey, and Detroit, Michigan, exploded in devastating riots.

President Johnson set up a commission, the National Advisory Commission on Civil Disorders (also called the Kerner Commission), to study the causes of the riots. After months of study, the commission charged white people in the United States with racism. It predicted that the United States would end up with two separate, hostile societies if things did not change. The president did not like the report of his own commission.

The SCLC went on with its work in Chicago. Two large grocery corporations agreed to carry products of black companies and to deposit the money earned in black neighborhoods in black banks. Jesse Jackson, then Martin Luther King's representative in Chicago, announced that Operation Breadbasket, which focused on jobs, would be tried nationally.

〰

Many people who were close to King began to notice a change in him. "He's angry," they said. "He's frustrated by the movement and disappointed with the president."

Both King and some of his aides felt that he was being stalked. They knew he could be killed at any time, in the midst of any crowd. One morning while he was preaching at his church in Atlanta, Martin said, "Every now and then I think about my own death, and I think about my own funeral...." Another time he said, "I thought I would be killed in Mississippi. I didn't think I would live to leave Mississippi."

〰

King began planning a Poor People's March to Washington because he thought the United States had forgotten about their problems. He said, "We will place the problems of the

Although he was tired and discouraged, King planned a Poor People's March in Washington, D.C.

poor at the seat of government of the wealthiest nation in the history of mankind.... All too often in the rush of everyday life there is a tendency...to overlook the poor, to allow the poor to become invisible...."

He thought the Poor People's March would have a dramatic effect on Congress. He wanted guaranteed jobs for those who could work, an end to housing discrimination, and he wanted the laws providing for integrated education to be enforced.

Although Dr. King was tired and discouraged, he wanted to find a way to organize the working poor—cleaning persons, garbage workers, seasonal workers—into unions. "Our challenge," he wrote, "is to organize the power we already have in our midst."

While King traveled around the country giving speeches and winning support for the Poor People's March, trouble was brewing in Memphis, Tennessee. Employees of the Memphis sanitation department were among the poorest paid and the most mistreated in the country. Their hours were long, collecting and hauling garbage was physically difficult and dirty work, and the workers had no job security or insurance. Dissatisfaction grew among the workers until one day they could no longer tolerate their situation.

On Wednesday, January 31, it rained in Memphis and drenched the city. After two hours of work, the garbage workers, most of whom were black, were sent home. On Friday, when they got their paychecks, the black workers found less than their usual pay. When they asked about it, they were told that they had only worked two hours the previous Wednesday instead of the usual eight. Since they were paid very low wages, $1.70 an hour by one account, the deduction would hurt and make it difficult to pay bills. But the black workers thought the deduction was fair until they talked to some white workers and learned that the white workers had been paid for a full day's work.

Memphis sanitation workers were members of Local 1733, a chapter of the American Federation of State, County, and Municipal Employees, but the city refused to recognize the union as a bargaining agent. The black workers knew they had been treated unfairly. Money wasn't the main issue; racism was.

Henry Loeb, the mayor of Memphis, refused to listen to the grievances of the black workers. On February 12, Local 1733 declared a strike. Mayor Loeb said, "If you don't come back to work, you'll lose your jobs." He didn't think the strike would last, but he didn't understand how angry black people had become. The black workers began to express what they felt. "We are tired of working for such low wages when we still have to shiver in cold shacks during the winter and swelter in the summer's heat. We work very hard, but we are still so poor that we can't feed our children or buy them the clothes they need. We are tired—tired of all of it."

And so the sanitation workers stayed home while the trash piled up in people's yards. "Do something," cried the citizens of Memphis. But their elected officials would not talk to the strikers. Instead, nonunion workers, escorted by police, collected the garbage from white neighborhoods.

James Lawson, Martin's old friend from the early marches in Alabama, marched with more than 1,300 employees who carried signs that read I AM A MAN. The march was peaceful until the police broke it up with nightsticks and Mace (an irritant that causes temporary blindness and skin rash). The black community became so angry that a strike-support group was organized. Shouting, "Freedom for our brothers," its members staged daily marches from the Masonic Temple to City Hall.

Lawson telephoned Martin, who was in Mississippi organizing his Poor People's March. He explained the dangerous situation in Memphis and asked Martin to come for a rally on March 18. Dr. King was torn between his duties, but he agreed to make the trip. He thought the situation in Memphis was a good example of what the Poor People's March was all about.

Martin was moved by the enthusiasm of the crowd at the rally. The audience sang, clapped their hands, and someone called out, "The King is here." When he spoke, he felt filled with fire as he had at the beginning of the movement. He told 15,000 people, "You have assembled for more than 30

Garbage piled up when
the Memphis sanitation
workers went on strike,
right. Their march,
above, was peaceful
until police broke it up.

King called for all black people in Memphis to join in a march.

days now to say, 'We are tired. We are tired of being at the bottom. We are tired of having to live in dilapidated, substandard housing.'"

Men, women, and children held up their hands and shouted, "Yes. That's right, brother."

King continued, "You are here to say, 'We are tired of working our hands off and laboring every day, and not even making a wage adequate to cover the basic necessities of life.' You are saying, 'We are tired of being emasculated, so that our wives and our daughters have to go out and work in white ladies' kitchens.'"

The crowd responded with applause and cries of "All right!"

"And so I say we aren't going to let any dogs or water hoses turn us around .... We've got to march again, in order to put the issue where it is supposed to be, force everybody to see that 1,300 of God's children are suffering, sometimes going hungry. . . ."

He called for all black people in Memphis to boycott their jobs for one day and join in a massive march. Thrilled by the support and enthusiasm he had seen, King decided to lead the march himself. He made this decision without knowing that there were Black Power advocates in that southern city. He felt safe in Memphis—so safe that when he left the city, he didn't leave any of his aides behind to organize the nonviolent march.

Had he attended a meeting with some local ministers and black youths, he would have been horrified to hear one young black man sneer at the idea of marching. "If you want honkies to get the message, you got to break some windows," he said. But Martin didn't know of the violence that lay beneath the surface of Memphis.

On March 21, a man with a husky voice called radio station WHBQ to warn, "If King returns to Memphis he will be shot."

Martin Luther King said, "... we aren't going to let any dogs or water hoses turn us around....We've got to march again...."

∽ TEN ∽

Free at Last
1968

"I just want to leave a committed life behind.
Then my living will not be in vain."
—Martin Luther King, Jr.

On Thursday morning, March 28, about 6,000 demonstrators assembled at Clayborn Temple in downtown Memphis. The march was supposed to begin at 9:00 A.M. A member of the Invaders, an organization of black militants, stood on the steps of the temple as the crowd milled around. "We gotta win a victory today," the activist shouted. "They burned down Watts and Detroit and Newark; man, we got to get into this, too. The black people ain't takin' this no more . . . ."

The day began hot and it grew hotter. Many young blacks were armed with sticks and carried signs that said BLACK POWER. They shuffled back and forth asking each other, "Where's King?" As time passed, they grew more and more irritated.

By the time King's plane had landed and he had been transported to the temple, the crowd was threatening to begin the march without him. Then someone shouted, "Here he comes."

King waved to the crowd as he hurried to the front of the line. "Let's go," his voice boomed. He linked arms with the marchers on either side of him. "Sorry I'm late," he said, and then he began to sing "We Shall Overcome." Soon hundreds were singing. The demonstrators had gone only three blocks when King heard a crash. He turned to see youths breaking windows and looting. Immediately he called, "Lawson, call off the march!"

"Go home!" James Lawson called through his bullhorn. "Stop the march! Turn around! Go back to your homes!"

The police had been parked in squad cars on adjacent streets. They quickly moved in. Tempers flared and fighting broke out. The situation suddenly became dangerous, and Lawson feared for King's life. "Martin!" he shouted through his bullhorn, "You've got to leave!"

Just then a car crossed Main Street. Quickly, an aide leaned in the window. "Madam," he said, "this is Dr. King—we need your car." In a moment King and Abernathy were being sped away to a motel.

Martin was exhausted. He sat on the edge of the bed and held his head. "We will return in two weeks," he said. "We must prove we can march peacefully before we go to Washington."

∽

While King was talking about peace and nonviolence, still another kind of trouble was brewing. James Earl Ray, who had escaped from Jefferson City Prison in Missouri, was preparing his own plan. On March 29, Ray, a white man with shell-rimmed glasses and a sharp nose, parked his white Mustang and walked into a store in Alabama called the

King was not prepared for the violence that broke out during the March in Memphis, but the police were ready.

Acromarine Supply Company. John DeShazo, a gun enthusiast, was leaning against the counter when Ray walked in. Ray was pale, had dark hair, and appeared to be in his early 30s. DeShazo noticed that Ray, dressed in a white shirt, dark tie, and wing-tip shoes, seemed to be out of place in the gun shop. He wanted to know what kind of rifle would be most accurate at a distance of 100 or 200 yards (91 or 183 meters). He was also interested in telescopic sights. Ray asked the clerk if he could look at a Remington Gamemaster, .243 caliber, an extremely powerful weapon.

Ray turned the gun awkwardly in his hands, then finally decided to purchase it. "Do you have a scope to fit this?" he asked. Thinking that Ray didn't know much about guns, DeShazo walked over to him and said, "You've really got quite a gun there. You'll have to learn how to use it."

Ray gave him a lopsided grin, bought a box of cartridges, and went to the street, where he climbed into his car and drove off.

DeShazo thought the customer had no business buying a rifle like that. "He's the kind of fellow who buys a rifle—probably to kill his wife."

The next day Ray exchanged the rifle for an even more powerful one, a 30.06.

On Wednesday afternoon, April 3, Ray climbed into his Mustang and drove down a stretch of U.S. highway from Birmingham, Alabama, to Memphis, Tennessee.

∽

While the Mustang was humming down the highway, Martin Luther King, Jr., and Ralph Abernathy were riding from the Memphis airport toward the Lorraine Motel with Reverend Lawson. When they stopped for a red light, a huge black hearse pulled alongside their car, and a black man leaned

At the Lorraine Motel on April 3, from left to right: *Hosea Williams, Jesse Jackson, Martin Luther King, and Ralph Abernathy*

out. "Reverend Lawson," he called. "Will you introduce me to Dr. King? I've never had the honor." After a brief introduction, the light changed, and the two cars moved on. Martin smiled, but he wondered if the hearse was a bad omen.

Later that day, Martin lay on his bed in room 306 of the Lorraine Motel as he talked with an SCLC member on the telephone. "You must cancel the march on Washington," his friend told him. "And if you don't get out of Memphis, you're going to get killed."

In the evening, King spoke before an audience of 2,000 followers at the Masonic Temple. When Abernathy presented him to the crowd, he said, "Tonight I'm going to introduce Dr. King with all the rights and honors he's entitled to." Later

*King talked about the situation in Memphis with SCLC aides
Andrew Young,* left, *and Hosea Williams,* center.

Abernathy said he had no idea why he did it, but he chose
that night to deliver what seemed like a eulogy, a speech
about a person that is usually given after his or her death.

When King walked to the podium, a great hush settled
over the auditorium, and he held his audience spellbound as
he traced events of the civil rights movement, his struggle,
his heartbreak, his climb to the mountaintop. He knew there
were some difficult days ahead, but, he said,

> ...it really doesn't matter with me now. Because
> I've been to the mountaintop....I have a dream...
> that the brotherhood of man will become a reality.

With this faith, I will go out and carve a tunnel of hope from a mountain of despair.... With this faith, we will be able to achieve this new day, when all of God's children—black men and white men, Jews and Gentiles, Protestants and Catholics—will be able to join hands and sing...the spiritual of old, "Free at last! Free at last! Thank God almighty we are free at last."

It was one of King's greatest moments, and the audience cheered enthusiastically.

By the next day, Thursday, April 4, tension was building in the city of Memphis. Hate literature was slipped under doors where white families lived. The White Citizens Council held a membership drive, and the Ku Klux Klan threatened to take to the streets if King marched.

At the motel, King and Abernathy called room service about 1:00 P.M. to have lunch brought to their room. They wanted catfish caught fresh from the Mississippi River, but the waitress made a mistake with the order and brought only one plate of fish instead of two. Abernathy wanted to send her back for the second plate, but Martin said, "That's all right. You and I can eat from the same plate." After lunch, Martin's younger brother, A.D. King, arrived and together they called their mother. Everyone's spirits were high all afternoon, and there was lots of laughter, hugs, and horseplay.

∾

That same afternoon, James Earl Ray checked into a shabby rooming house near the Lorraine Motel. His room had a green and gold plastic curtain hanging limply over a small, dirty window. There was a boarded-up fireplace, a sagging bed, and a filthy sofa with a greasy red pillow on it. In the center of the room hung a dim light bulb. The bathroom was at the end of the hall. From there, Ray had an almost perfect view of the Lorraine Motel.

∾

In room 306 of the Lorraine, Martin was standing in the bathroom getting ready to shave when there was a knock on the door. It was Reverend Samuel B. Kyles. King had accepted an invitation for dinner at the Kyles's home, and a limousine that had been borrowed from a funeral parlor waited below to transport King and his group.

King was in a jovial mood. He asked Kyles if his tie matched his suit. He joked about gaining weight because he was having trouble buttoning his shirt. He told Reverend Kyles that he had once gone to a preacher's house for dinner and they had served him Kool-Aid and cold ham. He was assured that Mrs. Kyles had prepared a prime rib roast and lots of soul food—chitterlings, greens, black-eyed peas, and pigs' feet. Ralph Abernathy wasn't quite ready, so Martin told him he would wait outside. Dr. King and Reverend Kyles stood at the iron railing along the motel balcony.

Some of King's aides were in the parking lot below. Andrew Young was visiting with Hosea Williams. James Bevel and James Orange were wrestling playfully. King called down to Bevel, "Don't let him hurt you." Then he spotted Jesse Jackson in brown slacks and a turtleneck sweater. "Jesse," King said. "I want you to go to dinner with us this evening. Be sure to dress up a little tonight."

"I am dressed," Jesse said. He had already been invited to the dinner.

A few minutes later, Reverend Kyles headed down to the parking lot, and King stood alone at the iron railing. Still in the room, Abernathy was standing in front of the mirror with aftershave lotion in his palms. He was just lifting his hands

Shocked aides pointed toward the source of the shot, as their leader lay dying at their feet.

up to his face when he heard a "pop" like a firecracker. A bullet had hit Martin Luther King, Jr., so violently that it had knocked him backwards. Abernathy ran to the balcony. "Oh my God!" he cried. "Martin's been shot!"

A nearby undercover policeman hurried to King's side. He tried to stop the flow of blood by pressing a towel against the wound. The bullet had torn away the right side of Dr. King's face and neck. Abernathy thought King seemed frightened. "Martin," he said, leaning close, "this is me. This is Ralph. Don't be afraid." King tried to speak, but only a faint murmur came from his mouth. Abernathy thought he could read his message: "I told you so." Andrew Young fell to his knees to see if he could find a pulse. He thought he found a faint beat.

A patrolman who had been watching the motel from the nearby fire station heard the shot and saw King fall. "Dr.

King's been shot!" he shouted. The fire captain called the radio dispatcher to send an ambulance. Two minutes later, the ambulance screeched into the courtyard.

"Up here," someone shouted from the balcony. "Bring the stretcher up here."

The ambulance driver shouted into his two-way radio, "Give me lights." All the traffic lights on the north and south streets were then set at green; all the others were red. This allowed the driver to speed to the hospital without stopping.

At the hospital, Ralph Abernathy walked beside the stretcher as Dr. King was taken to the emergency room. It pained Abernathy to see his friend suddenly look so small and helpless.

The doctors and nurses worked quickly under bright fluorescent lights. They tried to save King's life, but the bullet had done too much damage. His heartbeat began to fade. His heart beat slower, and slower, and slower, until finally, it stopped.

Martin Luther King, Jr., the man who had done so much to bring peace between different races, the man who had based his life on the practice of nonviolence, had been violently assassinated.

Outside the emergency room, Ralph Abernathy led a small group of friends in prayer: "We pray for the soul of Martin Luther King, Jr. May God in His infinite mercy bless him and keep his memory alive forever."

"I still have a dream.... that one day this nation will rise up and live out the true meaning of its creed, 'We hold these truths to be self-evident, that all men are created equal.'"

A farm wagon pulled by two mules carried Martin Luther King's coffin. Thousands of mourners followed.

EPILOGUE

Tributes and condolences were sent from all over the world. President Johnson declared Sunday, April 7, a national day of mourning, and all flags were flown at half mast. On Monday, April 8, the Memphis march that King had planned took place. Coretta and three of his children joined Ralph Abernathy to lead 30,000 people in the memorial march. Ten days later, the sanitation workers had their settlement and got everything they asked for: minimum wages, union representation, and benefits.

After the Memphis march, King's body was taken home to Atlanta, where it lay in state in the chapel at Spelman College. More than 1,200 mourners filed by each hour to pay their final respects.

Although King was not a head of state or a government official of any kind, his funeral was a stately affair. Vice-

President Hubert H. Humphrey, members of Congress, mayors from most major cities, foreign dignitaries, and a large number of distinguished private citizens attended his funeral. Eight hundred people squeezed into Ebenezer Baptist Church, and almost one hundred thousand more gathered outside.

After the church service, the pallbearers placed Martin Luther King's casket in a farm cart drawn by mules. It carried the martyred leader on his final march. A procession of mourners followed in the slow, sad walk to Morehouse College, where a public ceremony was held. King's body was then laid to rest in Southview Cemetery. The inscription on his monument reads: "Free at Last, Free at Last, Thank God Almighty, I'm Free at Last."

People were both sad and angry about the killing of Martin Luther King. While hundreds of thousands of people shed tears and vowed to work toward the fulfillment of King's dream, others burned and looted. Riots flared in more than 100 cities. Federal troops and the National Guard were called in. That King's death would cause so much violence was a cruel and bitter irony. Jacqueline Kennedy, the widow of President John Kennedy, asked "When will our country learn that to live by the sword is to perish by the sword?"

∽

President Johnson said, "The dream of Dr. Martin Luther King has not died with him. Men who are white, men who are black, must and will now join together as never in the past to let all the forces of divisiveness know that America shall not be ruled by the bullet, but only by the ballot of free and just men."

∽

James Earl Ray was captured at Heathrow Airport in London, England, two months after Dr. King's assassination.

*Stunned followers attended memorial services, which were held
throughout the country to mourn the slain civil rights leader.*

He pleaded guilty to first-degree murder and was sentenced to 99 years in prison. However, many questions about the killing remain unanswered, and many people believe that Ray did not act alone. They think that he was only a small part of a larger conspiracy.

～

Ralph Abernathy fulfilled King's wish for a Poor People's March on Washington. In May 1968, he led the march to dramatize the problems faced by poor people living in a wealthy country. King asked why millions of people suffered from poverty in a nation of such wealth. Much has been done in this area, but even more remains to be done.

Ralph Abernathy fulfilled King's wish by leading a march to dramatize the problems of poor people.

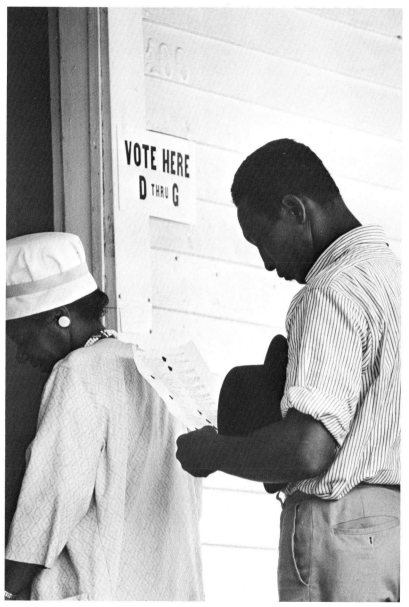

Because of King's courageous leadership, black people in the South are able to exercise their right to vote.

At Boston University, Coretta Scott King unveiled a memorial dedicated to her dead husband.

Martin Luther King, Jr., did not solve all the problems of racism and war and poverty, but he led the way toward peace, justice, and equality for all people. He didn't have all the answers. No one does. But he had faith that people were basically good, and he had hope for the future. Perhaps even more important, he shared his faith and hope. He led people to his mountaintop. He led them to see the world as it might be and to believe that, working together, they could change it.

In 1963, fewer than 50 black people held political office in the South, but with the Civil Rights Act of 1964 and the Voting Rights Act of 1965, black people entered the political arena. Now hundreds of black men and women hold political office. Several major cities, including Atlanta, Chicago, Los

Jesse Jackson, right, *was a candidate for the Democratic presidential nomination in 1984 and 1988. He is a civil rights activist, a political leader, and a Baptist minister. In 1990 he was elected an acting senator from Washington, D.C.*

Andrew Young, left, *was elected to the U.S. House of Representatives in 1972. He has also served as U.S. ambassador to the United Nations, and he was elected mayor of Atlanta, Georgia, in 1981 and reelected in 1985.*

The tomb of Martin Luther King, Jr., in Atlanta, Georgia. His memory lives on and the work that he began continues.

Angeles, and New York, have elected black mayors. Black people are members of Congress and state legislatures. In 1984 and 1988, Jesse Jackson was a candidate for the Democratic nomination for president of the United States.

∽

Martin Luther King was a great leader. To honor him and in memory of all that he accomplished, Congress declared King's birthday a national holiday. It is celebrated on the third Monday of January.

The memory of Martin Luther King, Jr., lives on, and the work that he began continues.

GLOSSARY

arraignment: the procedure in which a defendent is called before a court to answer to charges made against him or her

Black Power: the slogan of militant blacks; the use of the political and economic power of American blacks, usually to promote racial equality

boycott: the refusal to deal with a business or organization in order to express disapproval or force change

civil disobedience: the refusal to obey governmental demands; usually used as a nonviolent means of forcing concessions

civil rights: the rights of personal liberty guaranteed by law

desegregate: to eliminate the practice of isolating people according to race

discriminate: to treat one group differently than another based on something other than individual merit

Freedom Riders: civil rights workers who rode through southern states to see if public facilities such as bus stations had been desegregated

ghetto: the section of a city in which a minority group lives, usually because of social or economic pressure

grass roots: society at the local level rather than at the center of political power

integrate: to end segregation and bring about equality under the law

intimidation: the act of frightening through the use of threats

Ku Klux Klan: an organization advocating white supremacy

militant: aggressive; engaged in warfare

NAACP: the National Association for the Advancement of Colored People; a civil rights organization in the U.S. that works to end discrimination against blacks and other minority groups

nonviolence: the avoidance of violence as a matter of principle

racism: the belief that one race is superior to another

SCLC: the Southern Christian Leadership Conference; a civil rights organization in the U.S. that works to gain equal rights for black Americans and other minority groups through nonviolent civil protest and community development programs

segregation: the separation of one group of people from another, based on race or ethnic background

sit-in: the act of sitting in the seats of a racially segregated establishment in order to protest discrimination

SNCC: the Student Nonviolent Coordinating Committee (called Snick); a civil rights organization in the United States that existed during the 1960s. Under the leadership of Stokely Carmichael, it promoted the idea of Black Power.

stereotype: something conforming to a fixed or general pattern

zeitgeist: the general moral and cultural spirit of a particular era

For Further Reading

Abernathy, Ralph David. *And the Walls Came Tumbling Down.* New York: Harper & Row, 1989.

Bennett, Lerone, Jr. *What Manner of Man: A Biography of Martin Luther King, Jr.* Chicago: Johnson Publishing Company, Inc., 1968.

Bishop, Jim. *The Days of Martin Luther King, Jr.* New York: G. P. Putnam's Sons, 1971.

Branch, Taylor. *Parting the Waters: America in the King Years, 1954-63.* New York: Simon and Schuster, 1988.

Clayton, Edward T. *Martin Luther King: The Peaceful Warrior.* Englewood Cliffs, N.J.: Prentice-Hall, 1964.

Fairclough, Adam. *Martin Luther King, Jr.* Athens: University of Georgia Press, 1995.

Frank, Gerold. *An American Death: The True Story of the Assassination of Dr. Martin Luther King, Jr. and the Greatest Manhunt of Our Time.* Garden City, N. Y.: Doubleday & Company, Inc., 1972.

Haskins, James. *The Life and Death of Martin Luther King, Jr.* New York: Lothrop, Lee & Shepard Co., 1977.

Lewis, David L. *King: A Critical Biography.* New York: Praeger Publishers, 1970.

Oates, Stephen B. *Let the Trumpet Sound: The Life of Martin Luther King, Jr.* New York: Harper & Row, Publishers, 1982.

Preston, Edward. *Martin Luther King: Fighter for Freedom.* Garden City, N.Y.: Doubleday & Company, Inc., 1968.

Ralph, James. *Northern Protest: Martin Luther King, Jr., Chicago, and the Civil Rights Movement.* Cambridge: Harvard University Press, 1993.

Schulke, Flip and Penelope O. McPhee. *King Remembered.* New York: W. W. Norton & Co., 1986.

Washington, James Melvin, editor. *I Have a Dream: Writings and Speeches that Changed the World.* San Francisco: HarperSanFrancisco, 1992.

INDEX

Acknowledgments

The photographs in this book are reproduced through the courtesy of: J. Edward Bailey, III/NAACP, p. 52; Photograph Collections of the Birmingham Public Library, p. 26; Boston University Photo Service, pp. 22, 23, 116, 134; Dexter Avenue King Memorial Baptist Church, p. 25; the D.C. Public Library, pp. 45, 50, 84, 106, 108, 127, 131; Government of India, Ministry of Information and Broadcasting, Photo Division, p. 20; John F. Kennedy Library, p. 81; Martin Luther King Center for Nonviolent Social Change, pp. 12, 14, 19 (bottom); Library of Congress, p. 68; Y. Nagata, United Nations, p. 135 (bottom left); National Archives, pp. 60, 82 (bottom), 86; National Association for the Advancement of Colored People, p. 16 (all except bottom); National Rainbow Coalition, p. 135 (top right); Religious News Service, pp. 40, 49, 85, 88, 97 (bottom); Schomburg Center for Research in Black Culture, pp. 10, 16 (bottom), 43, 78, 121; Flip Schulke, pp. 1, 2, 6, 8, 9, 19 (top), 28, 36, 44, 46 (both), 51, 56, 58, 59 (all), 64, 65, 69, 70, 74, 75 (both), 80 (all), 82 (top left), 91, 92 (both), 94, 95, 97 (top), 98, 100, 103 (both), 105 (both), 110, 113 (both), 114, 119 (both), 122, 125, 133, 136; University of Mississippi, p. 101; UPI/Bettmann, pp. 62, 77 (both), 93, 128.

About the Author

Jean Darby received her Ph.D. from City University Los Angeles. She taught elementary school, grades pre-school through sixth, and has instructed college students in creative writing.

Ms. Darby has had more than 50 books for children published in the fields of science, beginning-to-read, picture books, social studies, and biography. She is the author of the Lerner biographies *Douglas MacArthur* and *Dwight D. Eisenhower*.

She has written numerous how-to articles for teachers and parents and writes a humorous newspaper column for grandparents. She lives in northern California and spends as much time as she can with her daughter and four grandsons.